BEYOND CHOPPED LIVER

BEYOND CHOPPED LIVER

59 Jewish Recipes Get a Vegan Health Makeover

by Kenden Alfond

JEWISH FOOD HERO

Nourishing your mind,
body and spirit

Library of Congress Cataloging-in-Publication Data

Names: Alfond, Kenden, author.
Title: Beyond chopped liver : 59 Jewish recipes get a vegan health makeover / Jewish Food Hero.
Description: Nashville : Turner Publishing Company, [2021] | Summary: "Beyond Chopped Liver: 59 Jewish Recipes Get a Vegan Health Makeover shares new and better ways to enjoy quintessentially Jewish food with delicious, plant-based recipes- from challah to matzo ball soup! The Jewish recipes in this cookbook are inspired by recipes from Jewish pre-modern Diaspora communities: Ashkenazi, Sephardi, Mizrahi, Beta Israel/Ethiopian and Indian Jewish communities, and from the modern Israel and American Jewish food cultures. The updates in this collection speak to the Jewish community today, as we seek to honor inherited Jewish food traditions, while living in ways that are healthier for our bodies and our planet. Communal meals are essential for family and community cohesion and health, and there should be no conflict between Jewish life and ethical eating. Offering healthier plant-based and vegan Jewish recipes is author, Kenden Alfond's way of problem solving and providing resources for the community, so that everyone can share delicious, healthy meals together"-- Provided by publisher.
Identifiers: LCCN 2020053660 (print) | LCCN 2020053661 (ebook) | ISBN 9781684425594 (paperback) | ISBN 9781684425617 (epub)
Subjects: LCSH: Jewish cooking. | Vegan cooking. | LCGFT: Cookbooks.
Classification: LCC TX724 .A44 2021 (print) | LCC TX724 (ebook) | DDC 641.5/676--dc23
LC record available at https://lccn.loc.gov/2020053660
LC ebook record available at https://lccn.loc.gov/2020053661

9781684425594 Paperback
9781684425600 Hardback
9781684425617 Ebook

Written by Kenden Alfond

Cover & book design by Rachel Mendelson

Printed in the United States

To the women in my family:

my grandmothers Bibby and Ellen,
my mother Joan,
and my daughter, Yaël

TABLE OF CONTENTS

INTRODUCTION

WHEN ONLY JEWISH FOOD WILL DO

There are times when it feels as though only Jewish food will do, either because it is a holiday and a specific food is called for, or because we want to be comforted by food that nourishes our memories. Foods we grew up enjoying have extra significance, due to the knowledge that our ancestors ate those same dishes.

Jewish food's "greatest hits" will endure, and my mission in this book is to give some of them a makeover. These updates speak to us today, as we seek to honour our inherited food traditions, while living in ways that are healthier for our bodies and our planet.

Communal meals are essential for family and community cohesion and health. Today I feel strongly that abstaining from meat and dairy should be socially acceptable in the Jewish community (and any community), at any family or communal meal. There should be no conflict between Jewish life and ethical eating. Offering healthier plant-based and vegan Jewish recipes is my way of problem solving and providing resources for our community, so that we can share delicious, healthy meals together.

JEWISH FOOD WAS AND IS INFLUENCED BY GEOGRAPHY

The "wandering Jew" is not just hyperbole. Jews have moved around a lot throughout Jewish history. Persecution and expulsion led Jews to leave established communities and form new ones; economic opportunities took individuals and groups from one location to another.

With the exception of modern Israel, Jews have always lived as minorities in other cultures, and their cuisine has been influenced by their geographic and cultural surroundings. For instance, Jews in Europe adopted the potato and milder seasonings, while Jews in the Middle East ate spicier foods based on grains and vegetables.

There are a few uniquely Jewish dishes. Cholent, Hamantaschen Cookies, and Matzo Ball Soup are examples of foods developed in order to fulfill Jewish laws and customs and are not found in other cultures. But most Jewish dishes arise from a collision between kosher food laws and local food habits and culinary traditions.

The two biggest Jewish communities today, in Israel and the United States, are a melting pot of Jews from all over the world. Additionally, the internet and television have democratized knowledge and made it easier for people to learn how to cook the traditional foods of other cultures.

You might go to Shabbat dinner in a Jewish home and enjoy a meal of Yemenite Soup, Challah, Mock Whitefish Salad , Pumpkin Patties, Israeli Salad with Bulgur and Chickpeas, and Fudgy Flourless Chocolate Cake—all on one table.

Jewish food and culture is today what it has always been—a multicultural affair. That, in my opinion, is cause for celebration.

JEWISH FOOD AND JEWISH RECIPES

Jewish food is not easy to define. Some foods are commonly eaten by Jews but have their origins in other cultures. Other recipes created by Jews were eaten by non-Jews as well. Then there are the foods traditionally eaten during Jewish holidays and during or after religious rituals, which may have been adopted from surrounding communities. Jewish food also means different things to people in different locations and time periods. For example, today Americans consider bagels to be a quintessential Jewish food, while Israelis barely eat them at all.

ENDURING TRUTHS THAT DEFINE JEWISH FOOD

- Jewish food and recipes adhere to Kosher laws.
- Jewish food has always been a multicultural affair because of the Jewish experience of migration.
- What Jewish people eat depends on where they live and where their ancestors lived.
- Shabbat and holidays have had a large effect on Jewish food. Foods that can be prepared in advance and heated up for a long time became popular for Shabbat dishes. Customs relating to specific holidays influence food choices.
- Not all foods considered Jewish food today are ancient in origin.

RECIPE SELECTION

The enormous diversity of Jewish food means this book can only show a small collection.

Jewish foods of greatest significance vary according to which culture and country we grew up in. The Jewish recipes in this cookbook are inspired by recipes from Jewish pre-modern Diaspora communities: Ashkenazi, Sephardi, Mizrahi, Beta Israel/Ethiopian and Indian Jewish communities, and from the modern Israel and American Jewish food cultures.

I was brought up in the United States and have been living overseas since 2005. How I think about food and communal eating has been heavily influenced and expanded as a consequence of my experiences living, cooking, and eating in other cultures. This has led to my growing interest in the evolution and diversity of Jewish food.

The recipes collected here are those that have inspired me over the past several years of eating and researching Jewish recipes. The selection covered here provides vegan versions of some classics, alongside a variety of recipes to diversify your table and meal rotation.

TERMS USED TO DESCRIBE JEWISH DIASPORA COMMUNITIES

The terms Ashkenazi, Sephardi, Mizrahi, Beta Israel, and Indian Jewish communities refer to the Jewish people that live and/or lived in geographically specific Diaspora communities, sometimes for centuries.

These terms are used today to refer to:

- an individual's unique ancestry and where their ancestors lived geographically;
- a Jewish group's unique way of "being" Jewish in history and in modern times—their rituals and interpretation of Jewish laws.

Ashkenazi: Jews whose ancestry can be traced to Central and Eastern Europe, namely Germany and Northern France. This group of people eventually spread out into other locations, including Poland, Russia, Latvia, Lithuania, and Belarus.

Sephardi: Jews from Iberia who scattered during the Spanish Diaspora in the years 1391–1492, migrating to Amsterdam, North Africa, and the Middle East.

Mizrahi: Jews whose ancestors lived in the Middle East, largely in Iraq, Iran, and Yemen.

Sephardi/Mizrahi: The terms Mizrahi and Sephardi are often used interchangeably to refer to all Jews whose ancestors lived in the Middle East and North Africa. In almost all cases I extended this logic to labeling the origin of recipes in this book. The only exception is the recipe for Yemenite soup, which is unique to the Yemenite community.

Beta Israel/Ethiopian: Jews who made mass migration from Ethiopia to Israel in the late 1980s and early 1990s.

Indian Jewish Communities: Jews whose ancestors lived in three communities, namely: Bene Israel, Baghdadi, and Cochin. Some of these communities claim to be Jewish immigrants to India in BCE, but mostly this label refers to 19th-century and 20th-century Sephardi or Ashkenazi immigrants to India.

There is and always has been racial and ethnic diversity in the Jewish community because of migration, intermarriage, and conversion. Today, many Jewish people can trace their ancestry to different communities and geographic locations.

PLANT-BASED AND VEGAN EATING CLARIFIED

In my quest to normalize animal product–free dishes at Jewish tables, one of the most accessible methods I have found is to simply add more plant-based dishes to every meal. There is no right or wrong way to enjoy more plant-based food, and indeed you don't have to identify as "vegan" or "plant-based," nor abstain from animal products 100 percent of the time in order to enjoy the dishes in this book! If you choose to serve a variety of these dishes alongside meat or dairy options, everybody benefits from more plant-based and vegan options on your table.

The recipes proposed in this book are all kosher pareve and are either plant-based or vegan. Nowadays, people might be confused about what the words "vegan" and "plant-based" actually mean—how are they different?

The term "vegan" refers to any food or product that doesn't contain anything from an animal or insect (meat, dairy, eggs, seafood, gelatin, whey, honey, etc.). Vegan does not automatically mean healthy. Oreos, processed breakfast cereals, diet coke, fruit leathers, and potato chips are all technically vegan.

"Plant-based" refers to any food or product made from the following five food categories: fruits, vegetables, tubers, whole grains, and legumes. A "plant-based" dietary pattern emphasizes eating mainly simple, unprocessed foods, avoiding the use of oils, and minimizing sugar, salt, and overt fats like avocado, coconut, and nuts.

Personal Dietary Patterns and Attitude

In reality, personal dietary patterns are unique. Some people eat vegan and plant-based all the time while most people eat vegan food and plant-based foods some of the time. Everyone has a different formula for achieving their version of optimal health, and for some people personal or environmental health are not a priority. For all of us, including more non-animal foods in our regular diet can only bring good. We will reap personal health benefits and positively impact the environment even if we simply reduce the amount of meat, fish, and dairy products we consume.

Regardless of how you eat, holding an extreme attitude in regard to food and health is not helpful or effective. Today, a healthy diet is coercively presented as something that is elusive and expensive to achieve, requiring specially grown foods, smoothies and a lot of complicated added superfoods, powders, and complex calculations. Nowadays our eating habits, what and where we buy our food, and how much we can afford to spend can be confused with our self-worth and personal goodness. Eating choices should not become one's whole life, nor should they create conflict with other people who choose to eat differently.

Four Primary Benefits of Eating More Plant-based Foods:

1. Feeling well: Eating minimally processed fruits, vegetables, tubers, whole grains, and legumes gives our bodies more fiber, complex carbohydrates, and water. All this supports the body to work the way it was designed to and allows us to feel satiated after eating.

2. Energy stability: Plants provide us with steady energy throughout the day. Forgoing energy spikes and crashes helps us experience mood stability. Think of a child fifteen minutes and an hour after eating a chocolate brownie and you can easily imagine how this works!

3. Environmental crisis: Food consumption impacts animals and our environment. In particular, land use and emissions from factory farming and other large-scale meat and dairy production contribute to climate change.

4. Disease prevention and treatment: Common health problems that can be prevented or improved by eating a plant-based diet include: diabetes, heart disease, obesity, acne, intestinal diseases, depression, fatigue, liver disease, kidney disease, high blood pressure, and more.

JEWISH ETHICAL PRINCIPLES AND FOOD CHOICES

The following four Jewish ethical principles are worth considering when making food choices.

Rachamim: Mercy and compassion

The Talmudic sages (Deuteronomy 11:22) inferred that acting with the divine traits of mercy and compassion is part of the commandment to follow in God's ways. In Judaism, this includes our relationships with other humans and with all living creatures. Mercy for animals is an integral part of Judaism.

Tza'ar ba'alei chayim: Do not cause animals unnecessary suffering

This instruction arises from a number of biblical commandments that are based on kindness to animals (Exodus 23:5, Deuteronomy 22:6–7 and 25:4, among others). Although the Bible permits the eating of meat, dairy, and fish, it places strict and specific regulations around animal treatment, slaughter, and consumption.

The original instruction is understood to prohibit causing unnecessary cruelty to animals, and to encourage positive actions to care for animal welfare. This commandment was given long before the mass production of meat, fish and dairy products. It falls on us to consider whether the Torah permits or condones the way animal foods are produced in modern factory farming, and the level of consumption of these foods today.

Choosing not to eat meat, fish and dairy, or simply reducing the amount you consume, reduces animal suffering.

U'Shmor Nafshecha: Guard Your Health

This instruction arises from Deuteronomy 4:9, which obligates us to take actions to guard our own life and prevent damage to our body. Eating well is one important action we can take to honor this instruction. Other important elements include: following safety laws and hygiene best practices; maintaining healthy physical and mental/emotional routines such as getting proper rest and sleep; moving our bodies regularly; developing a positive attitude; and participating in supportive and loving relationships. When we are in good physical health, it places us in a better position to do good.

We should not confuse this principle with the modern "wellness" industry that proposes that we make our own wellness the ultimate goal of our lives.

Bal Tashchit: Do not destroy

Bal Tashchit is given in Deuteronomy 20:19–20.

This instruction can be understood to mean that our actions should protect the environment and that wasteful or destructive behaviors are ethically wrong.

Food production methods, daily eating choices, and food waste habits have a powerful impact on our environment, for better or for worse. Eating more plant-based foods and less meat, fish, and dairy is an effective way of minimizing our destructive impact on the environment and perhaps even rehabilitating our ecosystems. When taken on a broad scale, positive individual actions have a protective effect on the environment.

May these health makeovers of traditional Jewish recipes nourish your body, mind, and spirit. I'm so glad you're here.

To your health and inspiration,
Kenden

BREAD

CHALLAH: THE MODERN UPDATE

ORIGIN: ASHKENAZI

Traditional Challah

Challah is a braided, rich bread. It is normally pareve (i.e., no milk or dairy ingredients) so that it can be eaten with meat during holiday and Shabbat meals. Challah ingredients can include flour, eggs, sugar, oil or margarine, water, yeast, and salt. The bread is finished with an egg wash, which gives it its signature shine when baked. Challah can be braided or presented in a round shape.

Vegan Challah

We need a healthier challah! This vegan recipe is a make-over for the iconic Jewish bread. Egg replacer is used to bind, and yeast and baking soda give a perfect rise. A minimal amount of sugar provides just the right amount of sweetness. Finally, the recipe is oil-free and uses a surprising mixture of coconut milk and potato puree to create a moist crumb. I invented this by accident while recipe testing—I wanted to use apple puree but it was 5am and I only had a potato. I tried it and it works! It hits all the challah taste and appearance boxes: it smells like challah, tastes like challah, and pulls apart like challah. Best of all, it is healthier for our bodies and our planet.

Vegan Challah Bread Recipe Variations

- Chewy: add 1 cup of chopped raisins or cranberries at the end of step 5.
- Baked starch: use baked sweet potato puree or pumpkin puree to sweeten and give a yellow hue.
- Apricot jam: In step 10, roll the dough into two long thin rectangles and spread with ¼ cup of apricot jam and 2 tablespoons of applesauce. Roll each into a cylinder (like a Swiss roll) and then twist them together into a double helix shape.

Vegan Challah Bread

Prep time: 30 minutes + 3 hours for rising the dough

Cook time: 35–40 minutes

Serves: 8

Tools

- Baking sheet
- Baking spray
- Cutting board
- Fork
- Knife
- Large mixing bowl
- Measuring cups and spoons
- Parchment paper
- Pastry brush
- Prep bowls - three small
- Vegetable peeler
- Wooden spoon

Ingredients

- ⅓ cup (90 g) potato puree
- 1 ½ teaspoons yeast
- 1 teaspoon sugar
- ½ cup (120 ml) warm water
- 3 tablespoons coconut milk
- 2 teaspoons baking powder
- 6 tablespoons warm water
- 1 ½ tablespoons egg replacer
- 3 cups (375 g) all-purpose flour, plus more for kneading step
- 1 ½ teaspoons salt
- ¼ cup (50 g) natural cane sugar + 1 teaspoon for proofing stage

For the Maple Syrup Wash:
- 1 tablespoon maple syrup
- 1 tablespoon water

Instructions

1. Make the potato puree by peeling a medium potato, dicing it, and boiling it for 12 minutes. Mash with a fork and set aside to cool.
2. Proof the yeast: place yeast and 1 teaspoon of sugar in ½ cup of warm (not hot) water. Mix and leave to sit for about 10 minutes until it is foamy.
3. In a separate prep bowl, combine coconut milk, baking powder and 3 tablespoons of water. Set aside.
4. In another prep bowl, combine egg replacer with 3 tablespoons of water and set aside for at least 1 minute. Add ¼ cup more water if necessary to make the dough tacky.
5. Combine the flour, salt, and sugar in a large bread bowl.

6. Add the yeast, coconut milk, egg replacer, and the potato puree mixtures to the dry ingredients in the large bread bowl. Combine well using clean hands until a sticky dough forms.

7. Tip dough onto a clean floured surface and knead for 5 minutes. Add flour sparingly as needed.

8. Place dough into an oiled bowl, cover, and allow to rise for 2 hours.

9. Gently push the air out of the dough and divide into strands—two for a round challah and three for a braid. It is worth using a kitchen scale to make sure you have equal parts.

10. For a two-strand round challah: roll each strand into a long cylinder and twist them around each other to form a double helix shape. On an oiled baking sheet, arrange the dough twist into a spiral shape. Tuck the end pieces under.

11. For a three-strand challah braid: lay the strands side-by-side and pinch together at the top end. Braid and pinch to finish the end. Place on an oiled baking sheet.

12. Cover the challah with a clean cloth and allow to rise for 1 hour.

13. Preheat oven to 350°F (180°C).

14. Optional step: brush sparingly with a maple syrup wash. The aim is to add shine—too much will make your bread soggy.

15. Bake for 35–45 minutes until bread is golden brown.

SPELT POTATO CHALLAH

ORIGIN: MODERN JEWISH LIFE

Traditional Spelt Challah

Spelt is an ancient grain that has been rediscovered. Perhaps our ancestors were baking bread with it. Today, using spelt flour in challah is a part of a larger health trend to modernize challah. Many people find spelt easier to digest, and this is a valid reason to give spelt challah a try.

Spelt Potato Challah

This vegan spelt potato challah is soft and delicious. It has the same taste and pull-apart texture as a regular challah with a deeper golden-brown color and nutty smell from the spelt flour. The mashed potato gives moistness and a tender crumb, and we're using only a minimal amount of vegetable oil.

Spelt Potato Challah Recipe Variations

- Chocolaty: add 1 cup of chopped dark chocolate or dark chocolate chips into the dough before braiding
- Dried Fruit: fold 1 cup of raisins, dried cranberries, or chopped dried apricots into the dough before braiding
- Fall-themed: swap out the mashed potato for pumpkin puree and season the bread with pumpkin pie spice

Spelt Potato Challah

Prep time: 3 1/2 hours

Cook time: 30 minutes

Serves: 1 bread

Tools

- 1 small bowl
- 1 measuring jug or a medium mixing bowl
- 1 large mixing bowl
- Measuring cups
- Wooden spoon
- Parchment paper
- Rimmed baking sheet

Ingredients

- 2 teaspoons dry active yeast
- 3 tablespoons + 2 teaspoons caster sugar
- ½ cup (125 ml) warm water
- ¼ cup (70 g) mashed potato
- ¼ cup unsweetened soy milk
- 2 tablespoons maple syrup or date syrup
- 2 tablespoons sunflower oil
- 3 ½ cups (440 g) spelt flour + more for kneading
- 1 teaspoon salt
- 1-2 teaspoons unsweetened soy milk, for brushing

Instructions

1. Add yeast, 2 teaspoons of sugar, and warm water to a small bowl and set aside for 5-10 minutes to allow the yeast to bloom and become foamy.

2. In the meantime, in a measuring jug or a medium bowl, combine mashed potato, soy milk, maple syrup, sunflower oil, and remaining sugar. Whisk to combine.

3. In a large mixing bowl, add in the spelt flour and salt; whisk briefly to combine.

4. Add the yeast mixture into the jug with the liquid ingredients and pour the mixture into the bowl with the flour. Combine with your hands until a sticky dough forms.

5. Tip onto a floured work surface and knead the dough for 5-6 minutes. Add flour, only a little at a time, if the dough sticks too much. Don't add too much flour - the dough should be slightly sticky.

6. Lightly grease the bowl you used to make the dough with some vegetable oil and place the dough into the bowl. Cover with plastic wrap and place in a warm spot to proof for 2 hours.

7. Divide the dough into 3 equal pieces and braid like a traditional challah.

8. Line a rimmed baking sheet with parchment and transfer the braided challah onto the prepared baking sheet. Cover with plastic wrap and leave to proof for another hour.

9. Preheat your oven to 350F/190C.

10. Lightly brush the dough with the unsweetened soy milk and place in the oven to bake for 25-30 minutes or until the challah is deeply golden brown. You'll know the challah is done when you knock on the bottom and it sounds hollow. Allow to cool for at least 40 minutes before serving.

KUBANEH

ORIGIN: YEMENITE

Traditional Kubaneh

Kubaneh is a Yemenite Jewish yeasted bread. Traditionally it is placed in a hot oven on Friday night, just as Shabbat starts. It stays there and is baked slowly overnight at a low temperature, then eaten on Shabbat morning. Kubaneh is made with flour, yeast, sugar and either butter or clarified butter. The dough is divided into portions, each of which is folded multiple times to create rose-like individual sized breads. The large quantity of butter used and this folding technique makes these breads similar to a croissant. However, unlike the croissant, individual Kubaneh are baked together in one dish so that they become pull-apart rolls. Sweet Kubaneh are made with sugar or honey syrups, while savory versions are served with tomato dishes or savory chutneys.

Vegan Kubaneh Bread

This vegan kubaneh bread recipe is lower fat as it omits dairy butter and uses a minimal amount or coconut oil or non dairy butter instead. The taste is still delicious, especially when it is warm and fresh out of the oven.

Variations

- Sweet: Make a simple sugar syrup from 2 tablespoons sugar, ¼ cup (60 ml) warm water and brush onto the bread 5 minutes before baking is completed.
- Seeds: Before baking, sprink 1 teaspoon sesame seeds and/or 1 teaspoon nigella seeds on top of the bread.

Vegan Kebuneh

Prep time: 2 hours

Cook time: 30 minutes

Yield: 10 rolls

Tools

- Large mixing bowl
- Measuring cups and spoons
- Plastic wrap
- Round baking pan

Ingredients:

- 1 ½ cups lukewarm water
- 1 sachet (7 g) dry active yeast
- 3 tablespoons castor sugar
- 4 cups all-purpose flour + extra, as needed
- ½ teaspoon salt
- 7 teaspoons coconut oil/non dairy butter

Instructions

1. Combine water, yeast, and sugar in a large mixing bowl. Set aside for 5 minutes to let the yeast activate - the mixture will get bubbly and foamy.

2. Add half of the flour to the yeast mixture and combine using a wooden spoon. Slowly add the remaining flour and salt, gently kneading the dough by hand. If it feels too sticky after the full 4 cups, continue adding flour, a tablespoon at a time, until the dough comes together in a smooth ball. It should still feel slightly sticky.

3. On a lightly floured surface, knead the dough for 8–10 minutes to activate the gluten. Roll the dough into a ball.

4. Grease the bowl you used to mix the dough with a teaspoon of coconut oil and the dough, swirling it around the bowl so it gets greased on all sides. Cover the bowl with plastic wrap and a clean tea towel and let the dough rest for an hour or until doubled in size.

5. Grease a round baking pan with a teaspoon of coconut oil.

6. Punch out the air from the dough and divide into 10 small balls. Roll out each ball into a thin disk using your hands. The dough will tear slightly in some places—don't panic, it will turn out OK!

7. Spread ½ teaspoon of coconut oil or non dairy butter onto each disk of dough and roll like a jelly roll. Fold each jelly roll like a rose and transfer to the prepared cake pan. Repeat with all 10 balls.

8. Cover the kubane with plastic wrap and set aside for a final proof of 30 minutes.

9. Preheat the oven to 350°F (175°C).

10. Bake the kubane for 30 minutes, uncovered. Leave to cool slightly before serving.

NO–KNEAD FERMENTED RYE BREAD

ORIGIN: ASHKENAZI

Traditional Rye Bread

Rye bread is a type of bread made with various proportions of all-purpose flour and flour made from rye grain. Traditional Jewish rye bread varieties include light rye, pumpernickel, and marbled rye bread. The leavened dough is sometimes seasoned with whole caraway seeds and finished with an egg wash.

No-Knead Fermented Rye Bread

This easy, no-knead recipe produces a hearty and chewy bread loaf that's full of robust rye flavor. You don't need any effort for this bread—just a little time to let the dough ferment and develop the gluten. It is a healthy homemade bread recipe that you can feel good about eating.

No-Knead Fermented Rye Recipe Variations

- Add-ins: fold some pumpkin seeds, sunflower seeds, slivered almonds, or chia seeds into the dough before baking.
- Sweetness: double the maple syrup and fold some raisins or dried cranberries into the dough.

No-Knead Fermented Rye Bread

Prep time: 24 hours

Cook time: 1 hour

Serves: 6–8 (one large loaf)

Tools

- Dutch oven
- Large mixing bowl
- Measuring cups and spoons
- Parchment paper
- Wooden spoon

Ingredients

- 3 cups (360 g) all-purpose flour (or white whole-wheat flour)
- 3 cups (300 g) dark rye flour, plus more for dusting
- 1 teaspoon dry active yeast
- 3 teaspoons salt
- 2 ½ (600 ml) cups water
- 3 tablespoons olive oil (optional, but it gives a good flavor)
- 3 tablespoons maple syrup
- 1 ½ tablespoons caraway seeds (optional)

Instructions

1. In a large mixing bowl, combine all-purpose flour, rye flour, yeast, and salt. Slowly pour in the water, olive oil, and maple syrup while mixing with a wooden spoon. Continue mixing until all of the flour is moistened and a sticky yet firm dough forms.

2. Cover the bowl with plastic wrap and let the dough sit out for 12–18 hours. The longer you leave out the dough, the better flavor it will develop.

3. Place a large sheet of parchment paper on your work surface and generously dust with rye flour. Transfer the dough onto the floured parchment and gently fold it onto itself to form a dough ball. Don't work it too much—you want to keep the air bubbles inside.

4. Sprinkle the top of the dough with a good bit of flour and cover with a clean tea towel. Let the dough rise for another 1–2 hours or until doubled in size.

5. Preheat your oven to 450°F (230°C) and place a covered Dutch oven on the center rack in the oven.

6. Once the Dutch oven is piping hot, carefully remove it using oven mitts and quickly invert the dough into the pot. Use the tea towel to help you while handling the dough. Be careful as the dutch oven will be really hot. Sprinkle the caraway seeds on top, if using.

7. Transfer the bread to the oven to bake for 30 minutes, covered. Uncover and bake for another 15–20 minutes, or until bread is nicely golden and crusty on top.

8. Remove the pot from the oven and carefully lift the bread out and transfer to a cooling rack to cool completely before slicing and serving.

YAEL'S STOVETOP PITA

ORIGIN: MIZRAHI

Traditional Pita

Pita is a yeast-leavened, round flatbread with a puffy pocket, commonly eaten in the Middle East and neighbouring countries. It is made with flour, olive oil, yeast, salt, and a touch of sugar so that the yeast ferments.

Yaël's Stovetop Pita

My daughter learned how to make stovetop pita bread at school and then taught us how to make it at home. It is incredibly easy and a fun activity to do together—I'm not kidding when I say that we all squealed with joy when the pitas puffed up in the pan. In Yaël's version, we reduced the amount of oil and added some whole-wheat flour. Once you have eaten pita fresh from the pan you will never want to eat store-bought again.

Pita Recipe Variations

Vary the flavors toward the end of step 4:
- Crunch: Add chopped pumpkin or sunflower seeds to add texture, flavor, and nutrition.
- Sweetness: Add chopped raisins or currents, orange zest, or ½ teaspoon of cinnamon.
- Savory: Add chopped baked garlic and ½ teaspoon of turmeric for a savory, golden pita.

Yaël Pita Bread

Prep time: 10 minutes + 2 hours for rising the dough
Cook time: 20 minutes
Serves: 8

Tools

- Cast-iron skillet
- Clean kitchen towel
- Large mixing bowl
- Measuring cups and spoons
- Rolling pin
- Sharp knife

Ingredients

- 2 ½ cups (300 g) all-purpose flour divided, plus extra for kneading
- 1 ½ cups (360 ml) lukewarm water, divided
- 1 ½ teaspoons active dry yeast
- 1 teaspoon light brown sugar
- 1 cup (125 g) of whole-wheat flour
- ½ teaspoon salt
- 1 teaspoon canola or olive oil

Instructions

1. Combine 1 cup of all-purpose flour and 1 cup of lukewarm water with all of the yeast and sugar in a mixing bowl. Mix with a fork.

2. Cover with a kitchen towel and allow to ferment for 30 minutes until thick and frothy.

3. Add 1 cup of all-purpose flour and 1 cup of whole wheat flour, ½ cup of lukewarm water, and salt. Fork mix until a sticky dough comes together.

4. Transfer to a clean floured surface and knead for around 10 minutes, gradually adding ½ cup of flour and a teaspoon of olive oil. The dough will become smooth and springy to the touch.

5. Shape dough into a ball and place in a mixing bowl. Cover with a kitchen towel and allow to rise for 1 hour or until it doubles in size.

6. Tip the risen dough onto a floured surface and knead for 1 minute. Use a sharp knife to cut into 8 to 10 equal pieces and form each into a ball with your hands.

7. Cover and allow to rise for another 30 minutes.

8. Roll each ball into a flat circle, cover, and allow to rise for another 30 minutes.

9. Lightly oil the skillet and heat over medium heat for 2 minutes.

10. One at a time, cook pitas in the hot skillet for 1–2 minutes each side until they puff.

DIPS AND SPREADS

HARISSA SPREAD

ORIGIN: SEPHARDI / MIZRAHI

Traditional Harissa

Traditionally, harissa is a type of oily spiced chili tomato paste. Its main ingredients are roasted red peppers, tomato paste, a hot pepper like serrano, olive oil, garlic, and spices. It is used as a flavoring paste during the cooking process or as a spicy condiment for cooked food.

Plant-based Harissa Spread

This healthier plant-based recipe delivers all the intense flavor in a lighter, more versatile spread packed with plant-based protein. Enjoy this spread on crackers, breads, vegetables , or to accompany rice or potatoes.

Harissa Spread Variations

- Texture: add about ¼ to ½ cup of walnuts to the dip; pulse to partially blend, leaving some chunky parts for texture.
- Spice: use chile de arbol or a couple of teaspoons of chili powder for a more intense heat.

Harissa Spread

Prep time: 15 minutes
Serves: 8

Tools

- Food processor
- Medium bowl
- Plate
- Serving dish
- Small frying pan
- Spatula
- Wooden spoon
- Measuring cups and spoons

Ingredients

- 2–3 large dried chiles (optional)
- ½ tablespoon cumin seeds
- 1 teaspoon coriander seeds
- ½ teaspoon caraway seeds
- 1 14 oz. (400 g) can cannellini beans
- 1 10 oz. (280 g) jar fire-roasted red peppers, drained
- 2 garlic cloves
- 2 tablespoons tomato paste
- 2 tablespoons lemon juice
- ½ tablespoon apple cider vinegar
- Salt to taste

Instructions

1. Add the dried chiles to a medium bowl and cover with hot water. Cover with a plate and allow to steam for 10 minutes. Reserve the soaking water.

2. In the meantime, toast cumin, coriander, and caraway seeds in a dry frying pan over medium heat. They are ready when they begin to pop and become really fragrant, around 4 to 5 minutes.

3. Transfer the spices to a food processor and pulse to a fine powder. (Alternatively, you can skip the toasting process and use the same amounts of pre-ground spices.)

4. Add the cannellini beans, fire-roasted peppers, garlic, tomato paste, and rehydrated chiles to the food processor and blend until smooth and creamy.

5. Add the lemon juice, apple cider vinegar, and a large pinch of salt. Pulse to combine.

6. Adjust texture by adding a tablespoon of the chile soaking water at a time until you reach your desired consistency.

7. Place in the fridge to chill for at least 1 hour before serving.

8. Season to taste and serve with crudites and crackers.

HUMMUS

ORIGIN: SEPHARDI / MIZRAHI

Traditional Hummus

Traditionally, hummus is made with chickpeas, lemon juice, garlic, salt, and a large quantity of olive oil and tahini. These ingredients give a creamy heaviness, and make it a calorie-dense dip.

Plant-based Hummus

Instead of oil, grated peeled zucchini provides the moisture to make this smooth hummus, and an added bonus is that it adds fiber too. The quantity of tahini is reduced to just one teaspoon for creaminess. I use canned salt-free organic chickpeas as a labor-and-time- saving device—they blend easily and it means we can have hummus anytime without planning ahead.

Plant-based Hummus Variations

- Alter the protein: use edamame, lima, or butter beans instead of chickpeas.
- Add more flavor and color: add roasted red pepper or beets to deepen the flavor and color.
- Herbs: add cilantro or parsley for a bright and light flavor alternative.

Hummus

Prep time: 10 minutes
Yield: 2 cups+

Tools

- Blender
- Colander
- Measuring cups and spoons
- Serving bowls
- Silicone scraper (to clean the blender)

Ingredients

- 1 cup (150 g) grated zucchini
- 1 × 14 oz (400 g) can of chickpeas
- ½ teaspoon salt
- 2 garlic cloves
- ⅛ teaspoon chili powder
- 1 tablespoon of apple cider vinegar or fresh lemon juice
- ¼ teaspoon ground cumin
- 1 teaspoon tahini
- Paprika for garnish (optional)

Instructions

1. Peel and grate 1 cup of zucchini and set aside.
2. Rinse chickpeas well in cold water.
3. Blend the grated zucchini until it liquefies.
4. Add chickpeas, salt, garlic, chili powder, apple cider vinegar, ground cumin, and tahini to the blender and blend until smooth. You may need to pause to scrape down the sides occasionally.
5. Taste and adjust seasoning and spices.
6. Place in a serving bowl (or two). Serve immediately or cover and refrigerate for up to 2 to 3 days (it will taste better fresher).
7. Sprinkle with ground paprika before serving.

MOCK CHOPPED LIVER

ORIGIN: ASHKENAZI

Traditional Chopped Liver

Traditional chopped liver is a pâté made from calf, beef, or chicken liver. It includes onions, hard-boiled eggs, and schmaltz (rendered animal fat, usually chicken). Traditional recipes are extremely high in protein, fat, and cholesterol.

Mock Chopped Liver

This plant-based version of chopped liver is made with mushrooms and walnuts. It has a "meaty" taste and is light and fresh at the same time. It is best served with crunchy celery sticks, matzo crackers, or fresh toast.

Mock Chopped Liver Variations

- Protein: Add 1 cup of organic chickpeas in step 6 of the instructions.
- Heat: Add ½ teaspoon chili powder in step 7 of the instructions.

Mock Chopped Liver

Prep time: 20 minutes
Yield: 2 cups+

Tools

- Food processor
- Large skillet (9- or 10-inch)
- Measuring cups and spoons

Ingredients

- ¼ cup (60 ml) vegetable broth
- ½ cup (75 g) chopped onion
- 2 cloves garlic, minced
- ½ teaspoon sea salt
- 2 cups (150 g) button mushrooms, cleaned and sliced
- ½ cup (55 g) walnuts
- 1 teaspoon balsamic vinegar
- Sea salt and black pepper, to taste
- Fresh parsley for garnish

Instructions

1. In a large skillet, heat vegetable broth over medium-high heat.
2. Add the onion and garlic and sprinkle with sea salt.
3. Sauté gently for 10 minutes, adding a touch more vegetable broth if the onion begins to stick to the skillet.
4. Add mushrooms, another sprinkling of sea salt, and a little more vegetable broth if needed.
5. Cook and stir for 5 minutes or until the mushrooms have softened.
6. Place the cooked vegetables, remaining sea salt, walnuts, balsamic vinegar, and black pepper in a food processor
7. Blend until well-combined but not completely smooth.
8. Season to taste and place in a serving bowl.
9. Garnish with fresh parsley and serve with celery sticks and matzo crackers.

ROASTED EGGPLANT AND YELLOW PEPPER SPREAD

ORIGIN: ASHKENAZI

Traditional Eggplant Spread

This traditional Romanian eggplant dish is made from chopped roasted eggplant, olive oil, vinegar, and garlic. The original recipe is tangy and high in fat.

Plant-based Roasted Eggplant and Yellow Pepper Spread

This plant-based recipe is healthier and just as tasty. Olive oil is omitted as it is unnecessary; the dip is lighter and just as delicious without the oil. The recipe adds roasted yellow pepper, baked garlic, and shallots to deepen the taste. Both fresh lemon juice and white vinegar give a complex tangy taste. A tiny amount of chili powder uplifts the whole taste experience without making it spicy. Instead, the chili balances the sweetness from the eggplant and yellow pepper.

Roasted Eggplant and Yellow Pepper Spread

Prep time: 35 minutes
Yields: 2 cups, plus more

Tools

- Baking tray
- Cutting board
- Fork
- Measuring spoons
- Mixing bowl

- Serving bowls
- Sharp knife

Ingredients

- 2 medium eggplants
- 1 yellow pepper
- 1 shallot
- 4 garlic cloves
- 1 tablespoon fresh lemon juice
- 1 teaspoon white vinegar
- ½ teaspoon salt
- ¼ teaspoon chili powder
- Chopped green onion tops for garnish

Instructions

1. Preheat oven to 375°F (190°C).
2. Place whole eggplants, yellow pepper, and peeled shallot and garlic cloves on baking tray and bake until soft, 25 to 30 minutes.
3. Allow vegetables to cool for 10 minutes.
4. Peel eggplant. Discard the skin and place the soft interior into medium-sized mixing bowl and mash with a fork.
5. Add minced garlic, diced shallots, and yellow pepper to the mixing bowl.
6. Add lemon juice, vinegar, salt, and chili powder. Taste and adjust the seasoning accordingly.
7. Place in a serving bowl (or two) and smooth out the top so it looks pretty. Refrigerate if not serving immediately.
8. Garnish with a sprinkle of chopped green onion tops.

ROASTED PUMPKIN AND APPLE SPREAD

ORIGIN: SEPHARDI / MIZRAHI

Traditional Pumpkin Spread

Traditional Libyian pumpkin spread is made from pureed pumpkin, harissa spice blend, olive oil, and honey. The original recipe is tangy and high in fat.

Vegan Roasted Pumpkin and Apple Spread

This is an improvement on the taste and nutrition content of the original. Roasted pumpkin is used here—don't even think about using canned! Roasting the pumpkin, apple, and garlic gives a richer flavor. Instead of honey, whole apple gives sweetness. In place of harissa, tomato paste and additional spices give a bright taste. The dip is moistened with the natural water content of the ingredients, rather than added liquid. This recipe uses half a teaspoon of olive oil to coat the apple and pumpkin in the baking phase so that they stay moist during baking.

Roasted Pumpkin and Apple Spread Variations

- Protein: Add ¼ cup of white beans to the recipe to give it more body and boost the protein.
- Anise: Add ¼ teaspoon caraway seeds to the recipe to add a subtle anise/licorice background taste.
- Heat: Use chili powder instead of paprika to make this dip spicier.

Roasted Pumpkin and Apple Spread

Prep time: 40 minutes

Yield: 2 cups+

Tools

- Baking dish
- Blender
- Measuring cups and spoons
- Serving bowls
- Silicone scraper (to clean the blender)

Ingredients

- 3 cups / 1.2 pounds (500 g) of raw kabocha pumpkin pieces, diced large
- 1 medium apple, chopped into small pieces
- 3 garlic cloves
- ½ teaspoon olive oil
- 1 tablespoon fresh lemon juice
- 1 tablespoon non-dairy milk
- 1 teaspoon tahini
- ½ teaspoon tomato paste
- ¼ teaspoon ground cumin
- ½ teaspoon paprika
- ¼ teaspoon cinnamon
- ½ teaspoon salt
- Paprika to garnish (optional)
- Freshly chopped cilantro for garnish (optional)

Instructions

1. Preheat oven to 400°F (200°C).
2. Peel, de-seed, and dice the pumpkin and apple and place into a mixing bowl.
3. Add three garlic cloves and olive oil, and mix to coat.
4. Spread evenly on a baking tray and put in the oven for 30 minutes or until tender, turning occasionally to cook evenly.
5. Remove from the oven and allow to cool for 10 minutes.
6. Place baked pumpkin, apple, garlic, fresh lemon juice, non-dairy milk, tahini, tomato paste, ground cumin, paprika, and cinnamon in a blender.
7. Blend until smooth. Adjust seasoning and spices to taste.
8. Transfer to a serving bowl and refrigerate if not serving immediately.
9. Garnish with a sprinkle of ground paprika or freshly chopped cilantro and serve.

SOUP

COCONUT SORREL SOUP

ORIGIN: ASHKENAZI

Traditional Sorrel Soup

This is a humble soup that in its purest form is made from water or broth, sorrel leaves, and salt. Variations of this recipe use different and easier-to-find greens such as spinach or chard. Some add egg yolks or whole eggs. Rice or potatoes can be added for starch.

Plant-based Sorrel Soup

This plant-based sorrel soup stays true to its humble beginnings and offers a gluten-free, dairy-free, oil-free version that is full of flavor. The potatoes and parsnips make it hearty and filling, while the sorrel gives an earthy taste. The added coconut milk and fresh lemon juice make the soup creamy and refreshing all at the same time.

Plant-based Sorrel Soup Variations

- Protein: add a can of cannellini beans or chickpeas to the soup.
- Blend it: if you prefer a smooth and velvety mouthfeel, blend the soup with a stick blender or in batches using a regular blender.

Sorrel Soup

Prep time: 10 minutes

Cook time: 30 minutes

Serves: 4

Tools

- Cutting board
- Large soup pot
- Lemon squeezer
- Measuring cups and spoons
- Sharp knife
- Vegetable peeler

Ingredients

- 1 medium leek, diced
- 2 scallions, diced
- 2 small parsnips, peeled and diced
- 4 medium potatoes, peeled and diced
- ½ teaspoon dried thyme
- ½ teaspoon dried dill
- 1 quart (950 ml) water
- 4 bunches sorrel, thinly sliced
- ½ cup (120 ml) coconut milk
- 1 lemon, juiced
- Salt and pepper to taste

Instructions

1. Add the leeks and scallions to a large soup pot and place over medium heat. Add a splash of water and season with a small pinch of salt and pepper. Cook, stirring occasionally, until vegetables begin to soften, around 4 to 5 minutes.

2. Add in the parsnips, potatoes, thyme, and dill. Season with another small pinch of salt and pepper. Continue cooking for another minute.

3. Pour in water and bring the soup to a boil, then immediately lower the heat to medium-low, and cover with a lid. Let the soup simmer gently until the potatoes are fork-tender, around 15 to 20 minutes.

4. Add in the sorrel and continue cooking until the sorrel is wilted, around 5 minutes.

5. Pour in the coconut milk and remove from the heat. Season to taste.

6. Serve immediately, with a squeeze of lemon.

GOLDEN POTATO AND CELERY SOUP

ORIGIN: SEPHARDI

Traditional Golden Potato Soup

This Egyptian soup is golden, silky, and made with everyday ingredients: potato, celery, onions, garlic, and oil. Aromatic turmeric adds a bitter, orangey-ginger flavor and gives the dish its golden color.

Plant-based Golden Potato and Celery Soup

This version omits the oil and adds some additional flavor elements to enliven the taste.

One teaspoon of chili powder is added to complement the turmeric, celery brings a natural salty crunch, and diced apple adds a hint of sweetness. Finally, coconut milk boosts the silky texture and creamy taste.

Golden Potato Soup Variations

- Orange vegetables: Add 1 chopped carrot to bring more color.
- Add crunch: garnish the soup with ½ cup coarsely chopped and toasted walnuts.
- Warmth: Add ½ teaspoon of nutmeg to bring a warm spice.
- Texture: This soup can be served as-is or pureed smooth.

Tools

- Cutting board
- Large soup pot
- Measuring cups and spoons

- Potato masher
- Sharp knife
- Spatula / wooden spoon
- Stick blender

Ingredients

- 1 medium yellow onion, chopped
- 4 shallots, chopped
- 3 cloves garlic, minced
- 8 cups (1,920 ml) low sodium vegetable broth
- 5 medium to large Yukon Gold or red-skinned potatoes, peeled and cubed into 1-inch pieces
- ½ apple, diced
- 4 celery stalks with leaves, sliced small
- ⅓ cup (80 ml) coconut milk
- 1 teaspoon ground turmeric
- ½ teaspoon chili powder
- ½ teaspoon salt
- 2 lemons, cut into wedges
- Salt and pepper to taste

Instructions

1. In a large soup pot, gently saute the onion, shallot, and garlic in a little water until translucent, approximately 3 to 5 minutes.
2. Add vegetable broth, potatoes, diced apple, diced celery, coconut milk, turmeric, chili powder, and salt. Bring to a boil, then reduce to simmer for 25 minutes or until potatoes are fully cooked.
3. Either keep as-is, or mash or blend depending on desired consistency.
4. Season to taste and serve with freshly cut lemon wedges.

MATZO BALL SOUP

ORIGIN: ASHKENAZI

Traditional Matzo Ball Soup

Traditional matzo balls are matzo meal dumplings served in chicken stock, commonly enjoyed during the holiday of Passover. They are made with matzo meal, melted schmaltz (usually chicken fat), eggs, and salt.

Plant-based Matzo Ball Soup

In this version, plant-based matzo balls are served in a rich vegetable broth. The matzo balls are made with potato puree and baked, giving them a pleasing consistency that holds up well as they float in the rich onion-leek broth. Matzo balls are one of those special foods that are hard to reinvent. The classic taste and texture are so specific that most people are not interested in alternatives. With that said, my mother, our designated Passover matzo ball soup maker, made these with me and called them "pretty good."

Plant-based Matzo Ball Soup Variations

- Flavor and color: add 1 teaspoon of turmeric to the broth to add a vivid color and subtle bitter flavor to the broth.
- Matzo Nuggets: during Passover, serve these as a crispy "matzo nugget" dipped in your favorite sauce (ketchup, tahini dressing, etc.).

Matzo Ball Soup

Prep Time: 1 hour 20 minutes
Yield: 15 matzo balls

Tools

- Baking dish
- Baking tray
- Chopping board
- Fine mesh strainer
- Fork
- Glass bowl
- Knife
- Large soup pot
- Parchment paper
- Small saucepan
- Soup bowls to serve
- Measuring and spoons

Ingredients

For the Soup Broth:
- 1–2 chopped onions
- 2–3 shallots, chopped
- 1–2 sliced leeks
- 2 cups (250 g) sliced carrots
- 1 turnip
- 1 bunch of parsley
- 1 tablespoon whole black peppercorns
- 10 cups (2,400 ml) water
- dill for garnish (optional)

For the Matzo Balls:
- 2 tablespoons cooked potato puree
- 1½ cups (180 g) matzo meal (or quinoa flakes to make gluten-free)
- ½ teaspoon sea salt
- ¼ teaspoon black pepper
- ½ teaspoon onion powder
- 1 ½ cups (360 ml) boiling water
- Baking oil spray

Instructions

Broth

1. Coarsely chop the vegetables and bake for 5 to 10 minutes at 450°F (220°C).
2. Transfer the baked vegetables to a pot, and cover with water by 2 inches.
3. Bring to a boil and reduce to simmer for 1 hour, adding more water as needed.
4. Strain the broth and set aside. Set the vegetables aside.

Matzo Balls

5. Boil a small potato, mash well with a fork, and set aside.
6. Combine the matzo meal (or quinoa flakes), sea salt, black pepper, and onion powder in a glass bowl.
7. Add ½ cup boiling water and potato puree and mix well.
8. Cover and refrigerate for 15 minutes.
9. Roll into walnut-size balls and place on a lined baking tray.
10. Lightly spray with oil and bake at 300°F (150°C) for 20 minutes, carefully turning midway through.

Assemble

11. Sweat the onion, carrot, and a pinch of sea salt in the soup pan for 10 minutes, adding broth as needed to prevent sticking.
12. Add the remaining vegetable broth, sea salt, and dill.
13. Bring to boil over medium-high heat, then simmer for 5 to 10 minutes.

To Serve

14. Place 3 matzo balls in each soup bowl.
15. Add the hot soup broth and garnish with dill.

RED LENTIL AND CHICKPEA HARIRA SOUP

ORIGIN: SEPHARDI / MIZRAHI

Traditional Harira Soup

A classic Moroccan soup enjoyed by the Jewish and Arab communities in Morocco. It is made with four essential ingredients: meat (beef, lamb or chicken), lentils, chickpeas, and tomatoes. The soup is sometimes thickened with eggs or a fermented flour and water mixture.

Plant-based Red Lentil and Chickpea Harira Soup

This delicious soup is oil-free, gluten-free, dairy-free, and full of plant-based protein and fiber. It is hearty, perfectly spiced, and has a good balance of textures from the chickpeas and red lentils.

Red Lentil and Chickpea Harira Soup Variations

- Lentil alternative: use brown or green lentils instead of red for different flavor and texture.
- Add creaminess: add ½ cup coconut milk in step 2 to make the soup creamy.
- Make it spicy: add minced red chili pepper or a few teaspoons of chili powder for a spicy kick.

Red Lentil and Chickpea Harira Soup

Prep time: 10 minutes

Cook time: 25 minutes

Serves: 4

Tools

- Colander
- Cutting board
- Garlic press
- Large soup pot
- Measuring cups and spoons
- Sharp knife
- Vegetable peeler
- Wooden spoon

Ingredients

- 1 yellow onion, diced
- 2 large carrots, peeled and diced
- 1 yellow bell pepper, diced
- 2 garlic cloves, minced
- ½ cup (95 g) red lentils, rinsed and drained
- 1 14 oz. (400 g) can chickpeas, rinsed and drained
- 1 14 oz. (400 g) can crushed tomatoes
- 1 teaspoon ground turmeric
- 1 teaspoon ground cinnamon
- 4–5 cups (960–1200 ml) water
- ½ cup (30 g) fresh parsley, chopped
- Lemon wedges, to serve (optional)
- Salt and pepper to taste

Instructions

1. Add the onions, carrots, yellow bell pepper, and garlic to a large soup pot. Season with a large pinch of salt and pepper and add a splash of water to stop them from sticking.

2. Place over medium heat and cook, stirring occasionally, until the onion becomes soft and translucent, around 4–5 minutes.

3. Add in the lentils, chickpeas, crushed tomatoes, turmeric, and cinnamon. Season with another pinch of salt and pepper.

4. Pour in water and bring the soup to a boil, then immediately lower the heat to medium-low and cover with a lid. Leave to simmer until the lentils are cooked through, around 15–20 minutes.

5. Remove from the heat and stir in the fresh parsley. Taste and adjust seasoning.

6. Serve with fresh lemon wedges.

SPICED YELLOW LENTIL SOUP

ORIGIN: SEPHARDI / MIZRAHI

Traditional Spiced Yellow Lentil Soup

This simple, spiced Iraqi soup combines yellow lentils with rice or broken angel hair pasta. It has a similar consistency to split pea soup and is golden yellow in color.

Plant-based Spiced Yellow Lentil Soup

This oil-free, creamy lentil soup stays true to its original form but with some minor improvements. A combination of tomato and tamarind paste is used to create a tangy acidic base. A rich spice blend makes the soup aromatic. Broken pasta pieces give a visual surprise. Serve with toasted bread for a really satiating meal.

Plant-based Spiced Yellow Lentil Soup Variations

- Easier spices: use a curry spice blend instead of the spices listed below.
- Vegetables: add diced carrot, celery, and tomato for added color and fiber.
- Bread instead: skip the pasta or rice and serve with fresh bread.

Plant-based Spiced Yellow Lentil Soup

Prep time: Overnight soaking of lentils + 12 minutes
Cook time: 30 minutes
Serves: 6–8

Tools

- Colander
- Cutting board
- Knife
- Large soup pot
- Measuring cups and spoons
- Soup pot
- Spatula / wooden spoon

Ingredients

- 1½ cups (300 g) split yellow mung bean lentils
- 1 medium white onion, chopped
- 3 shallots, chopped
- 3 garlic cloves, minced
- 10 cups (2400 ml) water or low-sodium vegetable broth (or a 50/50 mix)
- 1 tablespoon tomato paste
- 1 tablespoon tamarind paste
- 1 cup (120 g) chopped celery stalks
- 1 teaspoon cumin
- ½ teaspoon turmeric
- ½ teaspoon cinnamon
- ½ teaspoon chili powder
- ¼ teaspoon black pepper
- ½ teaspoon salt
- 2 bay leaves
- 2 oz. (60 g) angel hair pasta
- 2 lemons, cut into wedges
- Salt and pepper to taste

Instructions

1. Rinse yellow split peas in a colander several times. Place in soup pot and cover with plenty of water. Leave to soak overnight.

2. The next day, saute onion, shallots, and garlic in water for 3 minutes in a large soup pot.

3. Add broth, lentils, tomato paste, tamarind paste, celery, and all spices.

4. Bring to a boil then reduce to a simmer for 15 minutes, stirring occasionally.

5. Add uncooked broken spaghetti pasta pieces and cook for 10 minutes. Alternatively, cook the pasta separately and add it to the soup just before serving.

6. Serve with lemon wedges.

YEMENITE SOUP

ORIGIN: MIZRAHI

Traditional Yemenite Soup

Yemenite soup is a favorite for Shabbat dinners. The basic ingredients are a meat or chicken broth, marrow bones, onions, and potatoes. The special hawayej spice blend is made with cumin, caraway, coriander, turmeric, black pepper, cardamom, and cloves.

Plant-based Yemenite Soup

You won't miss the meat one bit with this delicious plant-based Yemenite soup. The tofu bulks up the soup with plant-based protein and its stringy texture is the perfect substitute for chicken. The traditional spice blend is perfect. This soup is both satisfying and comforting.

Plant-based Yemenite Soup Variations

- Tofu substitute: use tempeh or beans such as chickpeas or cannellini beans.
- More vegetables: add cubed zucchini or tomato to the soup for more flavor and texture.
- Turmeric broth: add 1 teaspoon of turmeric to the broth to give it a bitter medicinal flavor.

Plant-based Yemenite Soup

Prep time: 10 minutes

Cook time: 30 minutes

Serves: 4

Tools

- Cutting board
- Garlic press
- Large soup pot
- Sharp knife
- Spatula
- Vegetable peeler
- Measuring cups and spoons

Ingredients

- 1 yellow onion, diced
- 3 medium carrots, peeled and diced
- 2 garlic cloves, minced
- 1 ½ lb. (675 g) small potatoes, peeled and halved (or equal amounts large potatoes, diced)
- 8 oz. (225 g) firm tofu, torn into irregular pieces
- 1 teaspoon ground cumin
- ½ teaspoon ground turmeric
- ½ teaspoon ground coriander
- ¼ teaspoon ground caraway
- ¼ teaspoon ground cardamom
- 1 anise cloves
- 6–8 (1450–1900 ml) cups water
- ½ cup (30 g) fresh parsley, chopped
- 1–2 lemons, to serve (optional)
- Salt and pepper to taste

Instructions

1. Add the onions, carrots, and garlic to a large soup pot with a splash of water. Season and saute over medium heat until the onion becomes soft and translucent, around 4 to 5 minutes.

2. Add potatoes, tofu, and all the spices. Season with another pinch of salt and pepper. Add water and bring to a boil, then reduce to a gentle simmer and cover with a lid.

3. Allow to simmer until potatoes are fork tender, around 20 to 25 minutes.

4. Remove from heat and stir in the fresh parsley.

5. Ladle into bowls and serve with lemon wedges.

SALADS

BEET AND WALNUT SALAD WITH SPICED NON-DAIRY YOGURT

ORIGIN: SEPARDI / MIZRAHI

Traditional Beet Salads

Georgian beet salads are often paired with traditional walnut sauce, made from a thick puree of walnuts, red wine vinegar, onions, garlic, and spices like coriander, turmeric, hot paprika, and chili.

Beet and Walnut Salad with Spiced Non-Dairy Yogurt

This healthier beet and walnut salad is creamy, tangy, and slightly sweet all at the same time. This recipe highlights walnuts in their minimally processed state and is not as heavy as the traditional salad with walnut sauce. Balsamic roasted beets that melt in your mouth are the star of this salad. The spices of hot paprika and coriander are just enough to enliven the taste without making it too spicy. The chopped walnuts and dried cranberries add some texture and chewy sweetness, while the coconut yogurt rounds out the salad with a refreshing creaminess.

Beet and Walnut Salad Variations

- Herbs: trade the spices for dill to flavor the yogurt.
- More veggies: add some finely grated carrots and baby spinach to the roasted beet salad before serving.
- More sweetness: mix in some thinly sliced apples or pears for a sweeter salad.
- Protein: add a can of rinsed and drained chickpeas, white beans, or some cubed tofu to the salad for some plant-based protein.

Beet and Walnut Salad with Spiced Non-Dairy Yogurt

Prep time: 10 minutes

Cook time: 45 minutes

Serves: 4

Tools

- Cutting board
- Large serving dish
- Measuring cups and spoons
- Parchment paper
- Rimmed baking sheet
- Sharp knife
- Small bowl
- Spoon
- Vegetable peeler
- Whisk

Ingredients

- 4 medium beets, sliced
- 2 tablespoons balsamic vinegar
- ¼ cup (30 g) walnuts, roughly chopped
- 3 tablespoons dried unsweetened cranberries
- ¼ cup (15 g) parsley, chopped
- ½ cup (125 g) coconut yogurt
- 1 teaspoon fresh lemon juice
- ¼ teaspoon hot paprika
- ½ teaspoon ground coriander
- Salt and pepper to taste

Instructions

1. Preheat oven to 400°F (200°C).

2. Arrange the sliced beets on a lined baking sheet and season with a fat pinch of salt and pepper.

3. Roast until the beets are barely fork-tender, around 25 to 30 minutes.

4. Remove from the oven and lower the temperature to 350°F. Toss the beets with the balsamic vinegar and bake for another 10 to 15 minutes.

5. Once the beets are cooked and nicely glossy from the balsamic vinegar, remove from the oven and transfer to a large serving dish. Top with walnuts, cranberries, and fresh parsley.

6. In a small bowl, whisk the coconut yogurt with lemon juice, hot paprika, ground coriander, and a fat pinch of salt and pepper. Drizzle the spiced yogurt over the beet salad and serve on a large platter.

CARROT SALAD PLUS

ORIGIN: ASHENAZI AND SEPHARDI / MIZRAHI

Traditional Carrot Salads

Carrot salads are a favorite salad dish for Shabbat and Rosh Hashanah holiday meals. Usually, they feature cooked or raw carrots, herbs, olive olive or mayonnaise, and spices. They tend to be sweet, a bit one-note, and heavy because of the added olive oil or mayonnaise.

Plant-based Carrot Salad Plus

This carrot salad make-over offers a less sweet, healthier, and just as creamy salad. This salad features 3 other vegetables besides carrots: thinly sliced purple cabbage, romaine lettuce or spinach, and grated cauliflower. All these colors and flavors go together beautifully. The creamy dressing of tahini and plant-based milk is balanced by the acidic tang of mustard and vinegar.

Carrot Salad Variations

- Add sweetness: add raisins or diced dried apricots.
- Add seeds: add ½ cup of toasted sunflower seeds right before serving the salad to add crunch and more savory taste.
- More protein: add 1 cup of your favorite beans or quinoa to turn this protein-rich salad into a meal.
- Fresh herbs: add 1 cup of chopped parsley to the salad or as a garnish to increase the freshness.

Plant-based Carrot Salad Plus

Prep time: 10 minutes
Serves: 6

Tools

- Blender
- Box grater
- Cutting board
- Large spoon
- Measuring cups and spoons
- Salad bowl
- Serving spoons
- Sharp knife

Ingredients

- 3 cups (150 g) grated carrots
- 2 cups (180 g) thinly sliced purple cabbage
- 1 cup (115 g) grated cauliflower
- 3 cups (225 g) thinly sliced romaine lettuce or spinach leaves
- Salt and pepper to taste

For the Dressing:
- 3 garlic cloves
- 1 teaspoon salt
- 4 tablespoons white vinegar
- ½ cup (120 ml) rice milk
- 2 tablespoons tahini
- 2 tablespoons dijon mustard

Instructions

1. Add all dressing ingredients to a blender and blend until smooth. Set aside.
2. In a salad bowl, gently combine carrots, purple cabbage, and grated cauliflower.
3. Fold in the dressing and combine gently (no mushing the salad!).
4. Season to taste.
5. Serve on a bed of thinly sliced lettuce or spinach leaves.

CUCUMBER AND RADISH NON-DAIRY YOGURT SALAD

ORIGIN: SEPHARDI

Traditional Cucumber Yogurt Salad

Traditional Persian Mast o Khiar is a creamy dairy salad. Ingredients include yogurt, cucumbers, raisins, walnuts, and fresh herbs such as dill, chives, and basil. The special ingredient in this dish is rose petals. It is served as part of the Shavuot holiday meal as it features dairy.

Plant-based Cucumber and Radish Non-Dairy Yogurt Salad

This healthier cucumber and radish yogurt salad is dairy-free and uses plain plant-based yogurt. I used my mother's technique of leaving the cucumbers to sweat and drain for 8 hours to remove their high water content. I paired down the recipe to make it an everyday delight. Instead of three herbs, I like the simplicity of serving it with just one. The beauty of this recipe is that you can dress it up or down depending on what you are serving it with. This refreshing and delicious salad can be made up to a day in advance.

Plant-based Cucumber and Radish Non-Dairy Yogurt Salad Variations

- More tartness: add 1 cup of dried sour cherries.
- Add warmth: add ½ teaspoon each of cumin, curry, and turmeric to the dressing.
- Fruit: add in some thinly sliced-apples or pears for a sweeter salad.
- Texture: add ¼ cup of chopped walnuts and raisins.

Plant-based Cucumber and Radish Non-Dairy Yogurt Salad

Prep time: 4–8 hours (mostly waiting time)
Serves: 6–8

Tools

- Colander
- Cutting board
- Food processor
- Large salad bowl
- Measuring cups and spoons
- Sharp knife
- Vegetable peeler
- Wooden spoon

Ingredients

- 2.2 lbs (1 kg) peeled and thinly sliced cucumbers
- 1 teaspoon salt
- 1 cup (115 g) thinly sliced radishes
- 1 cup (250 g) non-dairy plain unsweetened yogurt
- 1 tablespoon white vinegar
- ¼ teaspoon ground pepper
- 2–3 garlic cloves, minced
- 1 cup (60 g) chopped fresh herbs (mint, dill, and coriander all work well)
- 6–10 green onions, thinly sliced

Instructions

1. Peel the cucumbers and slice them with a food processor's thinnest slicing blade
2. Place cucumbers in colander in the sink, add ½ teaspoon salt, and mix with your hands.
3. Slice the radishes with the food processor's thinnest slicing blade (no need to clean it) and place in a bowl in the refrigerator.
4. Allow to sweat for 4 to 8 hours in the sink.
5. Drain the cucumbers by squeezing the water out in small batches and place in a large salad bowl.
6. Add 1 cup of yogurt and combine gently.
7. Add vinegar, salt, and pepper, minced garlic, chopped fresh herbs of your choice, and green onion.
8. Taste and add more vinegar, salt and pepper to taste.
9. Can be served right away or chilled first.

ISRAELI SALAD WITH BULGUR AND CHICKPEAS

ORIGIN: SEPHARDI / MIZRAHI

Traditional Bulgur Salads

The most common ingredients in Israeli salad are chopped raw tomato, onion, and unpeeled cucumber. Sometimes, it is prepared with scallions and parsley. The most common salad dressing is olive oil and lemon juice.

Plant-based Israeli Salad

This bulked-up Israeli salad is hearty, fresh, and delicious. It is also oil-free. The added bulgur and chickpeas transform this side salad into a main dish. The usual cucumber, tomato, and fresh parsley bring in all of the freshness.

Israeli Salad Variations

- More vegetables: add finely diced green, red, or yellow bell peppers
- Bulgur substitutes: replace the bulgur with some cooked quinoa, millet, or brown rice.
- Dressing boosters: Add one tablespoon of tahini or ½ cup of plant-based plain yogurt to the salad for a richer dressing.

Israeli Salad with Bulgur and Chickpeas

Prep time: 30 minutes
Serves: 4 as a side

ANDE
MAI

xxxxxxx7590

2/9/2022

Item: ï¿½0010103178868 ((book)

Tools

- Citrus juicer
- Colander
- Cutting board
- Fork
- Large mixing bowl with lid (or plate to cover)
- Large spoon
- Serving bowl
- Sharp knife
- Measuring cups and spoons

Ingredients

- 1 cup (225 g) bulgur
- 1 ¼ cups (300 ml) of boiling water
- ½ cup (30 g) fresh parsley, chopped
- 1 lemon, juiced
- 3 scallions, thinly sliced
- 2 medium tomatoes, diced
- 2 small unpeeled cucumbers, diced
- 1 garlic clove, minced
- ½ teaspoon ground cumin
- 1 14 oz. (400 g) can chickpeas, rinsed and drained
- Salt and pepper to taste

Instructions

1. Place the bulgur in a large mixing bowl and season with a fat pinch of salt. Pour 1 ¼ cups of boiling water over the bulgur and cover with a tightly fitting lid. Set aside for 20 minutes.

2. Once the bulgur is soft but still chewy, fluff with a fork. Scatter on the fresh parsley and squeeze the lemon juice in. Stir to combine.

3. Add the scallions, tomatoes, cucumbers, garlic, cumin, and drained chickpeas. Season with a fat pinch of salt and pepper and give the salad a good toss.

4. Serve family-style or in individual portions. It tastes equally good served slightly warm from the bulgur or cold from the fridge.

MOCK WHITEFISH SALAD

ORIGIN: ASHKENAZI

Traditional Whitefish Salad

Traditional whitefish salad is a creamy affair. It is made with smoked white fish (lake whitefish, hake, sole, flounder, whiting, trout, cod, or sturgeon), mayonnaise, sour cream or crème fraîche, onion, and herbs.

Mock Whitefish Salad

This mock whitefish salad is made with chickpeas, vegan mayonnaise, silken tofu, plain coconut non-dairy yogurt, lemon juice, celery, smoked salt, and spices. The non-dairy, vegan mayonnaise combination gives the salad all the creaminess with less fat. Making the salad with smoked salt really gives it a similar taste profile to a traditional white fish salad. This salad is sure to become a family favorite, and it is especially delicious served as a topping on good toast.

Mock Whitefish Salad Variations

- Add heat: add ¼–½ teaspoon chili powder instead of black pepper. This rounds out the recipe and acts as a flavor enhancer. This is how I always make it at home.
- Add fresh garnish before serving: add ½–1 cup of chopped parsley or chopped green onion tops as a garnish before serving.
- Creaminess: add more of the non-dairy coconut yogurt and store-bought vegan sour cream to the recipe to boost the creaminess.

Tools

- Airtight container
- Citrus press
- Colander
- Cutting board
- Large spoon
- Measuring cups and spoons
- Salad bowl
- Sharp knife
- Silicone scraper (to clean the blender)

Ingredients

- ½ cup (125 g) plain unsweetened non-dairy yogurt
- 2 teaspoons lemon juice
- ½ teaspoon apple cider vinegar
- ½ teaspoon salt or smoked salt
- 2 14-oz.(400 g) cans chickpeas
- ¼ cup (60 ml) freshly squeezed lemon juice
- 2–3 garlic cloves, minced
- 2 shallots finely diced
- 2 cups (240 g) finely diced celery stalks
- 5 green onion tops finely sliced
- ¼ cup (60 g) vegan mayonnaise
- ⅓ cup (75 g) silken tofu
- ½–¾ teaspoon smoked salt (start with less and add more at the end to taste)
- ¼ teaspoon black pepper

Instructions

1. Rinse beans in cold water and place in a large salad bowl.
2. Squeeze fresh lemon juice and set aside.
3. Use your clean hands to mash the chickpeas until all individual beans are broken up—do not over-mush.
4. Add minced garlic, shallots, celery, and green onion tops to the bowl with the mushed beans.
5. Place vegan mayonnaise, non-dairy coconut yogurt, silken tofu, lemon juice, salt, and pepper into a blender and blend until smooth.
6. Gently fold the creamy dressing into the vegetables and beans (no mushing!).
7. Taste and season with lemon juice, salt, and pepper to taste.
8. Garnish with more green onion tops or fresh parsley.

POTATO AND SWEET AND SOUR CUCUMBER SALAD

ORIGIN: ASHKENAZI

Traditional Potato Salad

Traditional potato salad recipes include potatoes and either use an oil-based vinaigrette or mayonnaise dressing. Jewish versions of this salad sometimes include chopped boiled egg, sliced dill pickles, and a variety of vegetables and herbs.

Vegan Potato Salad

This recipe includes a vegan mayonnaise/silken tofu dressing that is just creamy enough without being heavy. Instead of kosher dill pickles, this salad uses Japanese-inspired homemade sweet and sour cucumber slices. Fresh radish, celery, and green onion bring vibrant fresh flavor and crunch. This recipe works best if you prepare the pickled cucumbers, dressing, and boiled potatoes a day in advance of assembling the salad. Refrigerating the separate ingredients overnight gives the pickles time to develop flavor, the dressing thickens, and the thoroughly chilled potatoes are easier to work with. Assembly the next day is quick and simple.

Vegan Potato Salad Variations

- Protein: add 1 cup of green peas to boost the protein in this salad.
- Kosher pickles: instead of the homemade pickle below, use store bought kosher pickles instead. Slice up 1 pickle and then add more to taste.
- Different vegetables: add thinly sliced cooked or raw carrots or beets to this recipe to boost the vegetables and color in the recipe.

- Dressing: instead of vegan mayonnaise and tofu, use ¼ cup each of tahini and plant-based milk in the dressing.

Potato and Sweet and Sour Cucumber Salad

Prep time: 25 minutes (and leave overnight)

Cook time: 15–20 minutes

Serves: 6–8

Tools

- Airtight container
- Blender
- Chopping board
- Colander
- Large spoon
- Measuring cups and spoons
- Prep bowl
- Salad bowl
- Saucepan
- Sharp knife

Ingredients

For the Pickles
- 1 lb (450 g) small cucumbers
- ¾ teaspoon salt
- ¼ cup (50 g) sugar
- 1 teaspoon soy sauce
- ⅔ cup (160 ml) rice vinegar

For the Dressing:
- ⅓ cup (80 g) vegan mayo
- 1 cup (225 g) silken tofu
- 4–5 garlic cloves
- 1 teaspoon Dijon mustard
- ½ teaspoon salt
- 1 teaspoon fresh lemon juice
- 1 teaspoon white vinegar
- 1 teaspoon rice vinegar
- ¼–½ teaspoon black pepper or chili powder
- 6 medium Yukon Gold potatoes or 4.4 lbs (2 kg) (peeled or unpeeled, your choice)
- 1 cup (115 g) sliced radishes
- 2 cups (240 g) thinly sliced celery
- 2 sliced green onions
- 2 cups (280 g) prepared cucumber pickle
- 15–25 green onions, sliced thin (both the green tops and white bulbs)

Instructions

1. Make the pickles: Thinly slice and salt cucumber. Allow to sit for 15 minutes in colander in the sink so they can sweat.

2. Squeeze out excess water and place in prep bowl. Add sugar, soy sauce, and rice wine vinegar, and mix. Ferment overnight by placing a weighted object in the prep bowl to submerge the cucumbers in the brine.

3. Make dressing: blend all dressing ingredients until smooth. Refrigerate overnight in an airtight container.

4. Boil whole potatoes in salted water (add 1–2 teaspoons salt to water) for 15 to 20 minutes until tender and then allow to cool for 10 minutes before placing in the refrigerator overnight.

5. The next day, 2–3 hours before serving (because it tastes best when the potato has time to marinate), cut the potatoes in half lengthwise, then cut into thick slices.

6. Drain the pickled cucumbers.

7. Place potatoes in a bowl and add pickled cucumber, sliced radishes, sliced celery, and sliced green onion.

8. Stir in dressing and combine gently. Allow to sit at room temperature or in the refrigerator before serving.

9. Season with salt, pepper, or vinegar to taste.

10. Garnish with green onion tops and serve.

PURPLE CABBAGE AND APPLE SALAD WITH TAHINI DRESSING

ORIGIN: ASHKENAZI

Traditional Purple Cabbage and Apple Dishes

Purple (or red) cabbage dishes are traditionally cooked and include the following basic ingredients: cabbage, apples, sugar, vinegar, red wine, and sometimes, apple juice. A variety of spices can be used, including cloves, bayleaf, or caraway seeds.

Plant-based Purple Cabbage and Apple Salad

This updated salad keeps the same basic nutrient-dense ingredients and presents them in raw, crisp, and crunchy form. The added roasted pumpkin seeds add a savory crunch. The creamy tahini dressing makes this raw vegetable and fruit salad delicious.

Purple Cabbage and Apple Salad Variations

- Juicier: add 1 cup of thinly sliced cucumbers in step 5.
- Sour: add ½ cup of prepared sauerkraut to increase the sour taste and health benefits.
- Fresh herbs: add ½ cup of chopped mint (or another favorite herb) to boost freshness.

Purple Cabbage and Apple Salad with Tahini Dressing

Prep time: 10 minutes
Serves: 6

Tools

- Blender
- Cutting Board
- Food processor
- Knife
- Prep bowls
- Salad bowl
- Measuring cups and spoons

Ingredients

For the Dressing:
- 3 garlic cloves
- 3 tablespoons tahini
- 4 tablespoons warm water
- ½ cup apple cider vinegar
- 2 teaspoons maple syrup
- 1/4 - 1/2 teaspoon xanthan gum powder
- ½ teaspoon salt
- ¼ teaspoon pepper

For Purple Cabbage and Apple Salad:
- 6 green onions chopped
- ½ cup of pumpkin seeds chopped
- 2 lbs (1 kg) purple cabbage thinly sliced
- 2 juicy and crisp apples, quartered and then thinly sliced or diced

Instructions

1. Add all dressing ingredients to blender and blend until smooth. Set aside.
2. Chop the green onions and set aside.
3. Chop the pumpkin seeds and set aside.
4. Slice cabbage with the food processor's thinnest slicing blade, place into a salad bowl, and massage with both hands for 3 minutes.
5. Slice the apple with the food processor's thinnest slicing blade (no need to clean it) and add to the salad bowl. If you prefer larger chunks of apple in this salad, dice it instead.
6. Fold in the dressing.
7. Season to taste.
8. Sprinkle the chopped pumpkin seeds and green onions on top. Serve as-is or gently mix to combine.

QUINOA HERB TABBOULEH

ORIGIN: SEPHARDI / MIZRAHI

Traditional Tabbouleh

Tabbouleh is a vibrant-looking and tasting finely chopped herb salad, packed full of fresh parsley, cucumber, tomato, onion, and bulgur. The salad is dressed with a generous quantity of olive oil, and lemon juice.

Quinoa Herb Tabbouleh

This tabbouleh is fresh and delicious, just like the original. The herbs are the focus here; they are the dominant ingredient and flavor. It is a vibrant green, speckled with red tomatoes and white quinoa and finished with a fresh lemon zing. Protein-rich quinoa replaces the usual bulgur. There is no need for oil in this salad; there is plenty of flavor from the herbs and vegetables, and the lemon juice dressing highlights the flavors perfectly.

Quinoa Herb Tabbouleh Variations

- Grain: use bulgur or millet instead of the quinoa.
- Spice: add cumin, paprika, or allspice to create a spicy tabbouleh.
- Protein: add a can of rinsed and drained chickpeas or white beans.
- Vegetables: add grated raw zucchini for an extra fresh vegetable taste and texture.

Quinoa Herb Tabbouleh

Prep time: 15 minutes

Cook time: 20 minutes

Serves: 4

Tools

- Large mixing bowl
- Medium saucepan
- Sharp knife
- Measuring cups and spoons

Ingredients

- 1 ½ cup (270 g) quinoa, rinsed and drained
- 3 cups (720 ml) vegetable broth
- 1–2 large bunches fresh parsley, finely chopped
- 1–2 small bunches fresh mint, finely chopped
- 2 medium tomatoes, diced
- 2 small cucumbers, diced
- 4 green onions, thinly sliced
- 3–5 tablespoons fresh lemon juice (to taste)
- Salt and pepper to taste

Instructions

1. Add quinoa and broth to a medium saucepan and season with salt and pepper. Bring to a boil, then immediately reduce to a gentle simmer and cover with a lid. Cook until the quinoa absorbs all the water and becomes fluffy, around 15 minutes.

2. Add the chopped herbs to a large bowl and add the warm quinoa on top. Mix with a fork until the herbs become really fragrant, around 1 to 2 minutes.

3. Add in the diced tomato, cucumber, and green onions; season with salt and pepper to taste. Toss with the lemon juice and place in the fridge to chill for 20 to 30 minutes before serving.

MAIN DISHES

BULGUR, SHIITAKE, AND WALNUT STUFFED PEPPERS

ORIGIN: SEPHARDI / MIZRAHI

Traditional Stuffed Vegetables

Many Jewish communities have their own version of stuffed baked or fried vegetable dishes. The general framework is vegetables or leaves stuffed with a grain and meat mixture, and then cooked in a sauce or fried in oil.

Plant-based Bulgur Stuffed Peppers

This plant-based version offers a healthier variation on the stuffed vegetable theme. These bulgur, shiitake, and walnut stuffed peppers are delicious and hearty. The combination of shiitake mushrooms, celery, raisins, walnuts, and miso provides the perfect balance between savory and sweet flavors, with plenty of chewy texture. Cooking the peppers in a miso broth on the stove top makes them plump and tender.

Plant-based Stuffed Peppers Variations

- Grain: replace the bulgur with rice, quinoa, and / or millet mixture.
- Protein: add crumbled tofu, tempeh, or even cooked brown / green lentils to the stuffing mixture.
- Baking: skip the stove top and use the same method to bake the peppers at 350°F (180°C) for 45 to 60 minutes.

Bulgur, Shiitake, and Walnut Stuffed Peppers

Prep time: 15 minutes

Cook time: 1 hour

Serves: 6–8 (1.5 to 2 stuffed peppers per person)

Tools

- Cutting board
- Large pot with lid
- Large skillet
- Sharp knife
- Measuring cups and spoons

Ingredients

- 3 shallots, diced
- 3 celery stalks, diced
- 2 garlic cloves, minced
- 1 lb. (450 g) shiitake mushrooms, chopped
- 2 cups (450 g) bulgur
- 2 teaspoons smoked paprika
- ½ teaspoon ground cumin
- ¼ teaspoon ground cinnamon
- 2 tablespoons miso paste
- ½ cup (80 g) raisins
- ½ cup (60 g) walnuts, chopped
- 10–12 large bell peppers (any color)
- 2–3 cups (480–720 ml) vegetable broth
- 2–3 spring onions, sliced (to serve)
- Salt and pepper to taste

Instructions

1. Heat a large skillet over medium heat and add in shallots, celery, garlic, and mushrooms; season with a pinch of salt and pepper. Add a splash of water so the vegetables don't stick, and cook, stirring occasionally, until soft with a bit of color, around 6 to 8 minutes.

2. Add in the bulgur, smoked paprika, cumin, and cinnamon. Season with another pinch of salt and pepper. Continue cooking, stirring constantly, until the bulgur becomes toasty and the spices fragrant, around 2 to 3 minutes. Remove from heat and stir in the miso, raisins, and walnuts.

3. Slice the tops off the peppers. Remove the seeds and set aside until next step.

4. Loosely fill each pepper with the bulgur mixture to about ¾ full. Don't overfill or the peppers will crack as the bulgur expands while cooking. Top with the sliced pepper tops.

5. Place the stuffed peppers in a large pot and pour in vegetable broth until it reaches around halfway up the peppers.

6. Place the pot over medium heat and let the broth come to a gentle simmer. Cover with a lid and cook until the bulgur is fluffy and the peppers are nicely soft, around 45 minutes.

7. Serve on a large platter and top with some sliced spring onions.

BUTTER BEAN COCONUT CURRY

ORIGIN: JEWISH INDIAN COMMUNITIES

Traditional Coconut Curry Dishes

Traditional Jewish Indian recipes are rooted in Kosher principles and are as varied as Indian regional cuisines. Alongside Indian spices, a consistent feature is the combination of coconut milk and Kosher meat: a creamy pairing permitted by Kosher food laws.

Butter Bean Coconut Curry

Instead of a meat dish with coconut milk and Indian spices, this delicate and creamy mild Indian curry is made with the "meatiest" of beans: butter beans. Also known as lima beans, they are naturally low in fat and high in protein. The recipe features diced chunks of succulent daikon radish, a common ingredient in South Asian cuisine. The spice profile is based on warm cinnamon, acidic fresh tamarind paste, chili, cumin, and beautifully golden turmeric.

Butter Bean Coconut Curry Variations

- Thicken: reduce the quantity of vegetable stock for a thicker coconut sauce.
- Soup it: add more stock for a beautifully spiced soup dish. This would be a perfect one-family one dish-meal that younger children might enjoy blended smooth.
- Pasta: add al dente linguine for a creamy Indian pasta dish. Trust me, this is delicious!

Butter Bean Coconut Curry

Prep time: 5 minutes

Cook time: 25 minutes

Serves: 6

Tools

- Blender
- Colander
- Cutting board
- Ladle
- Measuring cups and spoons
- Sharp knife
- Soup pot

Ingredients

- 1 onion
- 4 garlic cloves
- 1 14 oz. (415 ml) can coconut milk
- 3 cups (720 ml) vegetable broth
- 2 14 oz. (400 g) cans butter beans
- 1 cup (90 g) diced daikon radish
- 1 large potato, peeled and diced (optional)
- ½ teaspoon cumin
- ½ teaspoon coriander
- ½ teaspoon chili
- 1 teaspoon turmeric
- 1 teaspoon tamarind paste
- 1 cup (180 g) of de-stemmed collard green leaves sliced thin

Instructions

1. Gently saute the onion and garlic in a soup pot for 5 minutes.
2. Add coconut milk, vegetable broth, drained and rinsed butter beans, daikon radish, diced potato, and all the spices. Bring to a gentle boil.
3. Turn down the heat and simmer for 20 minutes.
4. Remove one ladle of broth and 10 butterbeans and add to a blender with the tamarind paste. Pulse until smooth.
5. Add the blended mixture back to the soup.
6. Add collard greens and simmer for 3 minutes.
7. Serve warm in soup bowls or on rice.

COCONUT BROWN RICE WITH PEAS

ORIGIN: COCHIN JEWISH COMMUNITY

Traditional Coconut Rice

Traditional coconut rice is a Southern Indian speciality popular in the area where the Cochin Jewish community lives. It is a pareve side dish featuring white rice, grated coconut, and shallots sauteed in clarified butter and fennel and fenugreek seeds.

Plant-based Coconut Brown Rice with Peas

This healthier brown basmati rice version skips the clarified butter. Grated coconut is extremely rich so a little goes a long way, hence the reduced quantity here. Green peas turn this side into a complete main dish. For convenience, I used ground spices and whole star anise to create a crowd-pleasing mild spice profile. With the crunch from chana dal, substantial plant-based protein and healthy fats of coconut and cashews, this rich, filling dish is best served with a fresh salad. Try pairing it with Cucumber and Radish Non-Dairy Yogurt Salad (p. 81).

Plant-based Coconut Brown Rice with Peas Variations

- White rice: if you prefer white rice, use white basmati to create this dish.
- Richer flavor: add 6 chopped shallots and stir fry in 2 teaspoons of vegan butter in step 2.
- Garnish: scatter chopped fresh coriander on top just before serving.
- Creaminess: serve with a dollop of vegan sour cream or yogurt.

Plant-based Coconut Brown Rice with Peas

Prep time: 10 minutes

Cook time: 15 minutes

Serves: 6

Tools

- Cutting board
- Frying pan
- Frying spatula
- Measuring cups and spoons
- Rice cooker
- Serving dish
- Sharp knife

Ingredients

- 3 cups (600 g) cooked brown basmati rice
- ¼ cup (38 g) cashew nuts
- 2 tablespoons chana dal
- 2 full star anise
- 1–2 whole dried red chili, sliced into large pieces
- 2 garlic cloves, peeled and halved
- 1–2 cups (85–170 g) grated fresh coconut meat
- ½ teaspoon salt
- ½ teaspoon chili powder
- ½ teaspoon ground cumin
- ½ teaspoon coriander
- 2 ½ cups (375 g) green peas

Instructions

1. Cook the brown rice (if you do not have a rice cooker, you should get one!)

2. Chop cashews into quarters and toast in a frying pan until slightly brown and the oils create a fragrant smell. Place in a prep bowl and set aside.

3. Toast the chana dal, star anise, chopped dried red chili, and garlic cloves in a frying pan over low heat until the chana dal becomes slightly brown and the spices fragrant.

4. Add the coconut and salt and toast for three minutes while gently stirring.

5. Add brown rice, chili powder, cumin, and coriander and stir fry for three minutes.

6. Add green peas and continue to stir fry for five minutes.

7. Remove the garlic and star anise and discard.

8. Garnish with the toasted cashew pieces and serve.

CRISPY BAKED FALAFEL

ORIGIN: SEPHARDI / MIZRAHI

Traditional Falafel

Traditional falafel is made from a paste of soaked and rinsed uncooked chickpeas, flour, garlic, onion, spices including cumin and coriander, and plenty of fresh parsley. The paste is formed into balls and deep fried in vegetable oil.

Plant-based Baked Falafel

This healthier falafel recipe stays true to the original. Baked rather than fried, the result is an oil-free, lighter take on a traditionally high-fat food. The falafels are crispy, tasty and seasoned to perfection. The fresher the raw chickpeas the better the texture and flavor. Double or triple the recipe and freeze the extras—simply heat in the microwave or in the oven for a quick lunch or dinner.

Crispy Baked Falafel Variations

- Switch out the beans: try fava beans or go bold with black beans in place of chickpeas.
- Sweetness: switch half the beans for sweet potato and stir in some raisins.

Crispy Baked Falafel

Prep time: 6 hours
Cook time: 40 minutes
Serves: 4

Tools

- High-speed blender or food processor
- Measuring cups and spoons
- Parchment paper
- Rimmed baking sheet
- Serving plate

Ingredients

- 2 cups (400 g) raw (dried) chickpeas, rinsed and soaked for at least 4 hours, preferably overnight
- 1 large onion, quartered
- 3 garlic cloves, peeled
- 1 lemon, juiced
- 1 teaspoon ground cumin
- 1 teaspoon ground coriander
- ½ bunch fresh parsley
- Salt and pepper to taste

Instructions

1. Preheat your oven to 400°F (200°C) and line a rimmed baking sheet with a piece of parchment paper.

2. To the bowl of a high-speed blender or a food processor, add the soaked and well-rinsed chickpeas, onion, garlic, lemon juice, cumin, coriander, and parsley. Season with a large pinch of salt and pepper and blend until a smooth mixture forms, around 1 to 2 minutes.

3. Use slightly wet hands to scoop up around 1 to 2 tablespoons of mixture and roll into small balls. Arrange the falafel balls on the prepared baking sheet.

4. Bake in the oven until deeply golden-brown on all sides, around 30 to 40 minutes. Flip once halfway through the baking time.

5. Leave to cool for a few minutes on the baking sheet before serving. Serve with pita bread and Harissa Spread and Israeli Salad with Bulgur and Chickpeas.

CRISPY BAKED TOFU SCHNITZEL

ORIGIN: ASHKENAZI

Traditional Kosher Schnitzel

Traditional kosher schnitzel is hammered kosher chicken or turkey, pounded thin with a meat tenderizer and then fried. The meat is usually dipped in matzo meal before frying, to give a crispy exterior.

Plant-based Baked Tofu Schnitzel

This crispy baked tofu schnitzel is crunchy on the outside and moist in the middle. It is dairy-free, oil-free, and vegan. With the combination of poultry flavor seasoning, the tofu takes on the texture and flavor of chicken. (Many people don't realise that most store-bought poultry seasonings are vegan.) Serve alongside mashed potatoes and Israeli Salad with Bulgur and Chickpeas.

Baked Tofu Schnitzel Variations

- Breading: replace the breadcrumbs with polenta or crushed corn flakes.
- Spice: switch out the poultry seasoning with some Italian herbs or chili powder for a spicy schnitzel.

Crispy Baked Tofu Schnitzel

Prep time: 45 minutes
Cook time: 40 minutes
Serves: 4

Tools

- Baking sheet
- Cooking spray (optional)
- Cutting board
- Heavy pan
- Measuring cups and spoons
- Parchment paper
- Sharp knife
- 3 Medium bowls

Ingredients

- 1 14 oz. (400 g) block extra firm tofu
- 7 tablespoons cornstarch
- ¾ cup (180 ml) unsweetened soy milk
- 2 teaspoons apple cider vinegar
- ½ cup (60 g) whole-wheat breadcrumbs or matzo meal
- ½ cup (70 g) Panko breadcrumbs
- 3 tablespoons nutritional yeast
- 2 teaspoons vegan poultry flavor seasoning
- Salt and pepper

Instructions

1. Slice the tofu block into 4 vertical slices. Wrap each in a piece of kitchen paper or a clean kitchen towel and place on a cutting board. Put a heavy pan on top and let the tofu press until most of the water comes out, around 30 minutes.

2. Next, prepare your breading station. Add the cornstarch to one bowl. In the second bowl, whisk the soy milk with the apple cider vinegar. In the third bowl, combine breadcrumbs, nutritional yeast, poultry seasoning, and a pinch of salt and pepper.

3. Preheat your oven to 400°F (200°C) and line a rimmed baking sheet with a piece of parchment paper.

4. Dip each tofu cutlet into the cornstarch first, then into the soy milk mixture. Repeat once, then finally, dunk the tofu into the breadcrumb mixture, making sure it is evenly coated on all sides. Transfer the breaded tofu to the prepared baking sheet and repeat with the remaining tofu pieces.

5. Spray the breaded tofu with cooking spray. This is an optional step, but it will make your tofu crispier.

6. Roast in the oven until nicely browned and crispy, around 40 minutes. Flip once halfway through.

7. Leave to cool for a few minutes before serving.

JACKFRUIT BRISKET

ORIGIN: ASHKENAZI

Traditional Brisket

Brisket is a cut of meat from the breast or lower chest of a cow. This tough cut of meat becomes tender and succulent after being slow cooked in a special sauce with onions, garlic, carrots, and potatoes at a low temperature for many hours. The sauce is the wildcard in every recipe and ranges from BBQ, sweet and sour, or red wine to Coca-Cola or coffee infused.

Plant-based Jackfruit Brisket

This jackfruit brisket is savory, slightly sweet, and delicious. It is meat-free and oil-free. In place of those heavy ingredients, we're using jackfruit—a tropical fruit with a meaty texture similar to that of shredded slow-cooked meat. The sauce is made from tomato passata, soy sauce, yellow mustard, and maple syrup.

Jackfruit Brisket Variations

- Texture: add thinly sliced shiitake mushrooms to make the jackfruit mixture more meat-like in texture and flavor.
- Spice: add minced red chili to the braising liquid for a spicy brisket.
- Serving ideas: serve with boiled or mashed potatoes and a green salad.

Jackfruit Brisket

Prep time: 10 minutes

Cook time: 40 minutes

Serves: 4

Tools

- Colander
- Cutting board
- Large pot
- Measuring cups and spoons
- Serving dish
- Sharp knife
- Whisk

Ingredients

- 2 cups (450 ml) tomato passata
- 3 tablespoons maple syrup
- 1 tablespoon apple cider vinegar
- 2 tablespoons soy sauce
- 1 tablespoon yellow mustard
- ¼ cup (60 ml) water
- 1 small onion, thinly sliced
- 2 garlic cloves, minced
- 1 teaspoon ground cumin
- 1 20 oz. (570 g) can jackfruit, rinsed and drained
- Salt and pepper to taste

Instructions

1. In a large pot combine passata, maple syrup, apple cider vinegar, soy sauce, mustard, and water. Whisk to combine.
2. Add in the onion, garlic, and cumin and season with a large pinch of salt and pepper. Place over medium heat.
3. Bring the mixture to a boil and add in the jackfruit. Reduce the heat to medium-low and cover. Let the jackfruit cook until you can easily shred it with a fork, around 30 to 40 minutes.
4. Use two forks to shred the jackfruit and transfer to a large serving dish.

LEMON, GARLIC, AND PARSLEY VARNISHKES

ORIGIN: ASHKENAZI

Traditional Kasha Varnishkes

Kasha Varnishkes is a heavy dish of pasta flavored with animal fat. It combines toasted kasha (toasted buckwheat groats) with farfalle (bowtie) pasta and onions fried in margarine or melted schmaltz (rendered chicken or goose fat).

Plant-based Kasha Varnishkes

This recipe offers a lighter, more flavorful and equally satisfying remake of this Jewish American favorite. It is oil-free, dairy-free, and high in fiber. The combination of garlic, lemon, parsley, and chili pepper really shines through, with a perfect balance of savory, tangy, and spicy flavors.

Plant-based Lemon, Garlic, and Parsley Varnishkes Variations

- Gluten-free: replace the whole-grain pasta with brown rice pasta for a gluten-free variation.
- Vegetables: stir some sautéed onions, peppers, mushrooms, greens, or even frozen peas through the pasta.

Plant-based Lemon, Garlic, and Parsley Varnishkes

Prep time: 10 minutes
Cook time: 15 minutes
Serves: 4–6

Tools

- Colander
- Cutting board
- Garlic press
- Knife
- Large pot
- Large saucepan
- Lemon juicer
- Measuring cups and spoons
- Medium pot
- Medium saucepan
- Serving dishes
- Skillet

Ingredients

- 1 cup (100 g) kasha, rinsed and drained
- 2 cups water
- ½ lb. (225 g) bowtie pasta
- 1 onion, diced
- 1 red chili pepper, deseeded and minced (leave the seeds in if you like it really spicy)
- ½ cup (30 g) parsley, chopped
- 1 lemon, juice and zest
- Salt and pepper to taste

Instructions

1. In a medium dry saucepan, toast the kasha over medium heat until you start to smell the nutty aroma. Pour over 2 cups of water and season with a large pinch of salt. Bring the water to a boil, then immediately reduce down to a simmer and cover with a lid. Cook until the kasha is plump and fluffy, around 15 minutes.

2. In the meantime, bring a large pot filled with water to a boil and season with a generous pinch of salt. Add the bowtie pasta and cook according to package directions.

3. While the pasta and kasha are cooking, add the diced onion to a skillet over medium heat with a pinch of salt and a splash of water to prevent sticking. Saute until the onions soften and develop a bit of color, around 6 to 7 minutes.

4. Add the red chili to the skillet and continue cooking until the chili becomes really aromatic, around 2 to 3 minutes.

5. Remove the skillet from heat and stir in parsley, lemon juice, zest, and season with more salt and pepper, to taste.

6. Mix the pasta with the kasha and the lemon parsley mixture. Toss to combine and serve immediately.

MINI SWEET AND SAVORY PARSNIP AND SWEET POTATO LATKES

ORIGIN: ASHKENAZI

Traditional Latkes

A classic Jewish holiday staple, latkes are crunchy potato fritters deep-fried in oil. Usually made with grated potatoes and matzo meal or flour, they can be seasoned by including onion and salt for a savory taste. They are served with a variety of toppings, popular ones including applesauce or sour cream.

Mini Plant-based Latkes

These latkes are mini-sized and baked, making them light and crispy. They are made with naturally sweet grated sweet potato and parsnip. Unlike traditionally greasy latkes, these are oil-free and healthier. I recommend you make two batches of this recipe because extras can be reheated or eaten cold the next day.

Mini Latkes Variations

- Sweet: serve with applesauce.
- Savory and protein: serve with tofu-based "sour cream".
- Ingredients: use white potatoes for a more traditional latke.

Mini Sweet and Savory Parsnip and Sweet Potato Latkes

Prep Time: 20 minutes

Cook time: 40 minutes

Serves: 4

Tools

- Baking sheet
- Box grater
- Fork
- Mixing bowl
- Oil spray
- Parchment paper
- Small saucepan
- Measuring cups and spoons

Ingredients

- 1 large sweet potato (or yam), coarsely grated
- 1 small sweet potato (or yam), mashed
- 1 parsnip, peeled and coarsely grated
- ¼ cup (30 g) all-purpose flour or gluten-free all-purpose flour
- ¼ teaspoon baking soda
- ½ teaspoon sea salt
- ¼ teaspoon black pepper
- 1 tablespoon low-fat non-dairy milk or water
- Cooking oil spray
- Toppings: Tofu Sour Cream & Chives or Applesauce (see recipes below)

Instructions

1. Boil the small sweet potato for 12 minutes, mash with a fork, and set aside.

2. Place grated raw sweet potato and parsnip in a mixing bowl.

3. Add flour, baking soda, sea salt, and black pepper and 3 tablespoons of the mashed sweet potato, stir to combine, and add the non-dairy milk or water.

4. Line a baking sheet with parchment paper and spray lightly with cooking oil

5. Use your hands to form balls from tablespoon-sized lumps of latke mixture. Flatten slightly to create patties.

6. Place the latkes on a lined baking sheet and bake at 350°F (180°C) for 25 minutes, or until golden on one side.

7. Flip gently and bake for another 15 minutes, or until golden brown.

8. Serve warm topped with either tofu sour cream and chives or applesauce.

TOFU SOUR CREAM

Yield: 1 cup

Tools

- Covered dish
- Food processor or blender

Ingredients

- 2 cups (450 g) silken tofu
- 1 tablespoon fresh lemon juice
- ½ teaspoon sea salt
- ¼ cup (15 g) finely sliced fresh chives

Instructions

1. Blend the tofu, lemon juice, and sea salt in a food processor until smooth.
2. Transfer to a dish, stir in chives, cover, and refrigerate until ready to serve.

APPLESAUCE

Yield: 3 cups

Tools

- Cutting board
- Knife
- Measuring cups and spoons
- Peeler
- Potato masher (or food processor)
- 4-quart saucepan

Ingredients

- 6 cups (720 g) apples, cored, peeled & diced
- 1 cup (240 ml) apple juice
- 1 teaspoon sea salt
- ½ cup (100 g) raw sugar or maple syrup
- 1 teaspoon cinnamon

Instructions

1. Place all ingredients in a 4-quart saucepan and bring to a gentle boil over medium heat.
2. Reduce heat to low, cover, and simmer for 25 minutes, or until apples are very soft.
3. Mash to a chunky texture by hand, or purée in a food processor.

MUJADARA

ORIGIN: MIZRAHI

Traditional Mujadara

This vegetarian Iraqi dish is popular all over the Middle East. Mujadara consists of lentils, grains, and onions and comes in an unlimited number of variations. The texture may be puree, pilaf, or porridge, the lentils can be brown or red, intact or mushed, and the grains can be groats, rice, or bulgur.

Plant-based Mujadara

This plant-based mujadara is a hearty dish filled with seasoned rice, lentils, and crispy, oven-baked onions. It is vegan, oil-free, dairy free, and absolutely delicious. Traditional mujadara is doused in oil; this lighter version allows the natural flavors of the ingredients to shine through.

Mujadara Variations

- Rice: switch white basmati for long-grain brown rice. Start by cooking the rice first for about 10 minutes, and then add in the lentils.
- Protein: add crumbled tofu or tempeh to the rice for extra protein.
- Creamy: pair the mujadara with coconut yogurt or Tofu Sour Cream (p. 134) for creaminess
- Heat: stir a little Harissa Spread (p. 35) through the finished dish to spice up the flavor.

Mujadara

Prep time: 10 minutes

Cook time: 40 minutes

Serves: 4

Tools

- Large pot
- Measuring cups and spoons
- Parchment paper
- Rimmed baking sheet
- Sharp knife

Ingredients

- 2 garlic cloves, smashed and peeled
- 2 bay leaves
- 5 cups (1200 ml) water
- 1 cup (200 g) brown lentils, rinsed and drained
- 1 cup (200 g) basmati rice, rinsed and drained
- 2 teaspoons ground cumin
- 2 large yellow onions, thinly sliced
- 1 tablespoon soy sauce or tamari
- ½ cup (30 g) fresh parsley, roughly chopped
- Salt and pepper to taste

Instructions

1. Add garlic, bay leaves, and water to a large pot and place over medium-high heat. Once the water starts to boil, pour in lentils and reduce the heat to medium. Cover with a lid and cook for 10 minutes.

2. After 10 minutes, uncover the lentils and stir in the rice and cumin. Cover and continue cooking until the rice is fluffy and the lentils are cooked but not mushy, around 20 to 25 minutes.

3. Meanwhile, preheat your oven to 400°F (200°C) and line a rimmed baking sheet with a piece of parchment paper.

4. Add sliced onions to the prepared baking sheet and season with soy sauce and a small pinch of salt and pepper. Place in the oven to roast until caramelized and dark brown all over, around 15 to 20 minutes.

5. When the lentils and rice are ready, fish out the bay leaves and mash the garlic cloves against the side of the pot with a fork. Generously season with salt and pepper to taste and gently mix to combine.

6. Serve the mujadara topped with crispy onions and fresh parsley.

MUSHROOM AND BARLEY MOLASSES CHOLENT

ORIGIN: ASHKENAZI (CHOLENT) AND SEPHARDI / MIZRAHI (CHAMIN)

Traditional Cholent

Cholent is the Ashkenazi name and chamin is the Sephardi / Mizrahi version of the slow cooked meat and bean stew usually served on Shabbat for the lunch meal. The recipe was developed in response to Jewish laws forbidding cooking on Shabbat. The cholent pot is started before Shabbat and continues to slow cook for 12 or more hours until lunch the following day. The common basic traditional ingredients of both cholent and chamin include meat, beans, vegetables, a grain or starch, and spices.

Plant-based Mushroom and Barley Cholent

This plant-based cholent is hearty and comforting. It is oil-free, dairy-free, meat-free and filled with plenty of vegetables, beans, and barley. It has all the familiar flavors of a traditional cholent while being healthier and filled with plant protein. If you cook with meat, making this dish with ¼ the amount of chicken or beef you would normally use will provide a meaty broth while reducing meat consumption.

Mushroom and Barley Molasses Cholent Variations

- Grain: use quinoa, millet, or buckwheat for a gluten-free cholent.
- Beans: switch out the kidney beans or chickpeas for white or black beans or red lentils.
- Texture: add crumbled tofu or tempeh to the cholent while cooking or top each bowl with some chopped walnuts.

Mushroom and Barley Molasses Cholent

Prep time: 10 minutes

Cook time: 8 hours

Serves: 6–8

Tools

- Crockpot
- Cutting board
- Ladle
- Large bowl
- Measuring cups and spoons
- Nylon (nut milk) bag
- Serving bowls
- Sharp knife

Ingredients

- 1 large onion, diced
- 2 large carrots, diced
- 1 lb. (500 g) white mushrooms, chopped
- 2 garlic cloves, minced
- 1 cup (180 g) raw kidney beans, soaked overnight
- 1 cup (200 g) raw chickpeas, soaked overnight
- 6 whole peeled medium potatoes
- ¾ cup (150 g) pearl barley
- 2 tablespoons molasses
- 1 teaspoon smoked paprika
- ½ teaspoon dried oregano
- ½ teaspoon dried basil
- 4–6 cups (960–1450 ml) warm water or vegetable broth (enough to cover the ingredients)

- ½–1 teaspoon chili powder (optional)
- Salt and pepper to taste

Instructions

1. Combine onion, carrots, mushrooms, garlic, kidney beans, chickpeas, and potatoes in a crockpot. Season with a large pinch of salt and pepper.
2. Put the barley in a nylon bag and place in the crockpot. The nylon bag will keep the barley grains separate while cooking.
3. In a large bowl, add about 1 to 2 pints of warm water or broth and stir in molasses, paprika, oregano, and basil.
4. Pour the water or broth over the ingredients in the crockpot. Add more water until the ingredients are covered.
5. Cook on low for 8 hours. Remove the nylon pouch and either stir the barley into the cholent or serve separately.
6. Ladle into bowls and top with fresh parsley.

PUMPKIN PATTIES

ORIGIN: MIZRAHI

Traditional Pumpkin Patties

This succulent dish is popular in Jewish and Arab cuisines in Syria, Turkey, and Greece. The traditional recipe uses bulgur, pumpkin puree, flour, coriander, allspice, cumin, and cayenne pepper. The mixture is formed into patties and pan fried.

Plant-based Pumpkin Patties

These oil-free plant-based pumpkin patties are simple to make and benefit from health improving adjustments. Instead of bulgur wheat or wheat flour, they feature gluten-free oats, which are high in protein. The flax seed used as a binder also gives a nutty taste. Mashed chickpeas provide protein and the spice mixture warms and has just enough fire to taste interesting without being too spicy. You can make them any size you like. These satisfying pumpkin patties can be made a day in advance and warmed up, so consider making a double batch. Serve with a fresh, crunchy green salad or lightly steamed greens.

Plant-based Pumpkin Patty Variation

- Sweet: replace the spice mix with cinnamon, add 2 tablespoons of brown sugar and top the finished patty with date syrup.
- Casserole: instead of patties, bake the mixture as a casserole in a 9″ lightly oiled baking dish. Can be made savory or sweet.
- Toppings: Serve with vegan sour cream or applesauce.
- Add more vegetables: add ¼ to ½ cup of minced leek and saute with the onion and garlic.

Pumpkin Patties

Prep time: 10 minutes

Cook time: 30 minutes

Yield: 9–12 patties

Tools

- Baking sheet
- Ice cream scoop or tablespoon
- Large mixing bowl
- Measuring cups and spoons
- Spatula
- Whisk
- 3 Medium prep bowls

Ingredients

- ½ sugar pumpkin to yield 2 cups (450 g of pumpkin puree)
- 1 tablespoon ground flax seeds
- ¼ cup (60 ml) water, divided
- 1 yellow onion, diced small
- ¼ cup (65 g) leeks, thinly sliced
- 2 garlic cloves, minced
- 1 cup (165 g) cooked chickpeas, mashed
- ½ cup (45 g) rolled oats
- 1 teaspoon salt
- ½ teaspoon ground coriander
- ½ teaspoon grated black pepper
- ¼ teaspoon ground allspice
- ¼ teaspoon ground cumin
- ⅛–¼ teaspoon cayenne pepper

Instructions

1. Halve the sugar pumpkin. Bake one half face down on a lined baking sheet in an oven preheated to 400°F (190°C) for about 40 minutes.

2. Add 1 tablespoon of ground flax seed and 2 tablespoons of water to a small bowl. Allow to sit for 10 minutes.

3. Remove the skin from the baked pumpkin, add the flesh to a bowl, and mash with a potato masher, hand-held blender, or fork. Ensure you have 2 cups of pumpkin puree.

4. Reset oven to 350°F (170°C).

5. Saute diced onion, thinly sliced leeks, and minced garlic for 3 to 5 minutes until soft and translucent. Add to the bowl with the mashed pumpkin.

6. Place chickpeas in a prep bowl; use clean hands to mash them . Add chickpeas and 2 tablespoons of water to the bowl with the pumpkin and onion.

7. In a large mixing bowl, combine the flax seed, rolled oats, salt, coriander, grated black pepper, ground allspice, ground cumin, and a pinch of cayenne pepper. Mix well.

8. Add the dry ingredients to the wet and stir until batter forms.

9. Form small patties in your hands, using 2 to 3 tablespoons of mixture for each. Place them on a lined, lightly greased baking pan.

10. Very lightly oil the tops of the patties, then bake for about 15 minutes, or until golden brown in color and firm.

11. Flip each patty and bake for another 10 to 15 minutes until golden brown.

SABICH SANDWICH

ORIGIN: MIZRAHI

Traditional Sabich

The classic sabich is a pita bread stuffed with slices of fried eggplant, hard boiled egg, and various condiments and vegetables. Originally an Iraqi recipe, nowadays, it is a favorite in Israel where it is served with the additions of hummus, Israeli salad and parsley. The stuffing is dressed with a combination of a mango pickle called amba, and a thin sauce of tahini, lemon juice, and garlic.

Healthier Plant-based Sabich

This plant-based sabich is healthy, fresh, and flavorful. Unlike the traditional method of frying the eggplant in oil, we're baking it until it crisps up. The harissa dip adds a good bit of spice to the sabich and the tabbouleh makes it fresh and zesty.

Vegan Sabich Variations

- Bread: serve the sabich in a whole-wheat bun, a tortilla, or piled on top of crunchy toasted bread slices.
- Protein: add a couple tablespoons of cooked chickpeas or white beans.

Sabich Sandwich

Prep time: 10 minutes

Cook time: 20 minutes

Serves: 4

Tools

- Large baking sheet
- Parchment paper
- Sharp knife
- Measuring cups and spoons

Ingredients

- 1 medium eggplant, washed
- ½ teaspoon garlic powder
- ½ teaspoon ground cumin
- 4 pita breads (½ batch Yael's Stovetop Pita Bread (p. 29)
- 6 tablespoons Harissa Spread (p. 35) (or plain Hummus p. 38)
- ½ batch Quinoa Herb Tabbouleh (p. 101)
- 4 medium pickles, thinly sliced
- 2 tablespoons vegan mayo
- Salt and pepper to taste

Instructions

1. Preheat your oven to 400°F (200°C) and line a large baking sheet with a piece of parchment paper.

2. Slice the eggplant lengthwise into 1-inch (2.5 cm) slices, then cut in half lengthwise again to make long stick shapes. Arrange the eggplant on the prepared baking sheet and season with garlic powder, cumin, and a generous pinch of salt and pepper.

3. Bake the eggplant until crispy around the edges and soft in the middle, around 20 minutes.

4. Spread 1½ tablespoons of harissa spread on the bottom of each pita pocket, followed by a couple tablespoons of tabbouleh. Top with 2 to 3 roasted eggplant pieces and sliced pickles. Finish with ½ tablespoon of vegan mayonnaise per sabich.

5. Repeat with the remaining pita pockets and serve immediately.

SPINACH-LEEK AND MASHED POTATO MATZAH MINA PIE

ORIGIN: SEPHARDI

Traditional Mina

Traditional mina is a layered savory matzah pie for the holiday of Passover, when consuming leavened products is prohibited. Ingredients include either ground meat or cheese with any vegetable and always mashed potatoes. The matzah pieces are dipped into broth to soften them before baking. An egg wash is applied to the top matzah piece to make it shiny and golden during the baking process.

Plant-based Spinach-Leek and Mashed Potato Matzah Mina Pie

This layered mina combines savory mashed potatoes with sautéed leek and either spinach or kale for a winning Pesach dish. It is the size of one matzo sheet and enough for four people. Double up if you have more than four people—but to keep it pretty, make any additional minas in separate baking dishes.

Plant-based Spinach-Leek and Mashed Potato Matzah Mina Pie Variations

- Fresh herbs: alter the herbs for a different flavor profile.
- Zingy: add one to two teaspoons of freshly squeezed lemon juice to the mashed potato.
- Glaze: instead of topping the mina with tomatoes, mix 1 tablespoon of maple syrup with water and lightly brush on the top matzo to mimic the egg wash effect of the traditional recipe.

Spinach-Leek and Mashed Potato Matzah Mina Pie

Prep time: 40 minutes

Cook time: 30 minutes

Serves: 4

Tools

- Baking dish
- Colander
- Cutting board
- Large bowl
- Large skillet
- Medium saucepan
- Potato masher
- Sharp knife
- Spatula for frying
- Vegetable peeler
- 8 × 10-inch baking dish
- Measuring cups and spoons

Ingredients

- 6 medium-size red skinned potatoes, peeled and cut into chunks
- ¼ cup (60 ml) vegetable broth
- 4 shallots, minced
- 2 leeks, sliced into half moons
- 2–4 cloves garlic, minced
- 1 tablespoon freshly sliced thyme leaves
- 6 large kale (or spinach) leaves, torn into bite-sized pieces
- 4 whole-grain or normal matzah sheets
- 3 ripe tomatoes, sliced extra thin
- Salt and pepper to taste
- Parsley sprigs for garnish

Instructions

1. Preheat the oven to 350°F (180°C).
2. Boil, drain, and mash the potatoes, adding enough vegetable broth to achieve a smooth consistency, somewhere between mash and puree.
3. Season to taste and set aside.
4. Saute the shallots, leeks, garlic, and thyme leaves for 3 minutes.
5. Add kale or spinach leaves. Remove from the heat as soon as they wilt—they will cook more during the baking stage.
6. Soak the matzo in a bowl of vegetable broth just long enough that they begin to soften (don't let it get soggy).
7. Lightly oil the baking dish and place a layer of matzo on the bottom.
8. Spread 1 ½ cups of the potato mixture evenly over the matzo.
9. Spread half of the leek-kale-spinach mixture on top of the potato layer.
10. Top with another matzo layer.
11. Repeat all layers. Finish with the fourth matzo, topped with thinly sliced tomatoes.
12. Bake for 30 minutes and allow to cool for 15 minutes before cutting and serving, garnished with parsley.

SPLIT PEA STEW

ORIGIN: BETA ISRAEL/ETHIOPIAN

Traditional Ethiopian Split Pea Stew

Kik Alicha is a traditional, simple, comforting stew often served with injera, a sour spongy flatbread that takes several days to make. Kik Alicha is made with yellow or green split peas, oil, onions, and traditional Ethiopian spices.

Plant-based Ethiopian Split Pea Stew

This plant-based stew omits the oil and offers a vibrant, delicious, and crowd-pleasing spice blend. Don't be tempted to add too much water during cooking—remember that this is a stew! The finished dish has a thick, flavorful broth. This stew is perfect to serve with rice, potatoes, flatbread, or Yael's Stovetop Pita Bread.

Plant-based Ethiopian Split Pea Stew Variations

- Easy spice option: use a high-quality, authentic pre-made berbere spice blend rather than the individual spices mentioned.
- More vegetables: add 2 cups of thinly sliced celery to add freshness to this stew.
- Creamy: add ¼ cup of full-fat coconut milk for a richer taste. This is my favorite variation of this recipe.

Tools

- Colander
- Large soup pot
- Wooden spoon
- Measuring cups and spoons

Ingredients

- 1 ½ cups (340 g) dry split green peas, soaked overnight
- 2 large red or yellow onions, diced
- 4 shallots, minced
- 2 tablespoons ginger, minced
- 1 jalapeno pepper, seeded and diced (optional)
- 2–4 garlic cloves, minced
- ½ teaspoon sweet paprika
- ½ teaspoon chili powder
- ½ teaspoon salt
- ¼ teaspoon cinnamon
- ¼ teaspoon coriander
- ¼ teaspoon turmeric
- ¼ teaspoon black or white pepper
- ¼ teaspoon allspice
- ⅛ teaspoon cardamom
- ⅛ teaspoon nutmeg
- ⅛ teaspoon fenugreek
- 6 cups (1440 ml) vegetable broth or water, divided
- Green onion for garnish

Instructions

1. Wash the split peas and place in a soup pot covered with plenty of water. Leave to soak overnight.

2. The next day, drain the split peas, rinse well, and set aside.

3. Saute onion, shallots, ginger, jalapeno, and garlic in large soup pot for 5 minutes.

4. Add beans and all the spices to the soup pot and mix for 1 minute.

5. Add 5 cups of vegetable broth and bring to a boil and then turn down to simmer for 20 minutes, stirring occasionally.

6. Taste to make sure the split peas are soft, and then depending on the stew consistency add 1 cup of vegetable broth.

7. Allow to sit for 15 minutes in the covered soup pot before serving because the split peas will continue to cook and absorb the broth.

8. Season to taste and garnish with chopped green onion before serving.

STUFFED CABBAGE ROLLS

Origin: Ashkenazi, Sephardi, Mizrahi

Traditional Stuffed Cabbage Rolls

Stuffed cabbage leaves follow the same general theme: cabbage leaves are separated and wrapped around a mixture of minced beef, rice, and spices. The sausage-shaped rolls are arranged in a Dutch oven, covered with tomato sauce, and then baked. Variation from community to community focuses on spicing and size, ranging from thin cigars to big, hearty rolls.

Plant-based Cabbage Rolls

These plant-based stuffed cabbage rolls are spicy and delicious. The tomatoey rice filling is fresh and all of the fragrant flavors from the herbs—mint, parsley, and dill—really shine through. Double the recipe and enjoy these hearty cabbage rolls as leftovers.

Plant-based Cabbage Roll Variations

- Protein: add tempeh, lentils, or chopped walnuts to the rice filling.
- Spice: add some smoked or hot paprika for a warmer-tasting cabbage roll.
- Grain: replace the rice with bulgur, millet, quinoa, or barley.

Stuffed Cabbage Rolls

Prep time: 45 minutes

Cook time: 1 hour

Serves: 6–8

Tools

- Colander
- Large plate
- Large pot
- Large skillet
- Measuring cups and spoons
- Sharp knife
- Tongs

Ingredients

- 1 large green cabbage
- 2 onions, diced
- 3 garlic cloves, minced
- 2 medium tomatoes, diced
- 3 tablespoons tomato paste
- 2 teaspoons ground cumin
- 1 teaspoon dried mint
- 2 cups (360 g) short-grain rice
- ½ bunch fresh parsley, chopped
- ½ bunch fresh dill, chopped
- 2 ½ cups (600 ml) vegetable broth
- Salt and pepper to taste

Instructions

1. Fill a large pot with water and add a generous pinch of salt. Place over medium-high heat.
2. Using a sharp knife, cut out the core from the cabbage. Place the whole, cored cabbage into the water and boil for 2 to 3 minutes.

3. Using tongs or forks, start removing the cabbage leaves from the pot, one by one, and transfer to a colander. Repeat the process until you have removed all of the cabbage leaves.

4. Wash the leaves under cold water and allow to drain thoroughly. Reserve a few cabbage leaves separately.

5. In the meantime, add the onion, garlic, and tomatoes to a large skillet and place over medium heat. Season with a pinch of salt and pepper and add a splash of water so they don't stick. Cook, stirring occasionally, until the vegetables become soft and translucent, around 5 to 6 minutes.

6. Add the tomato paste, cumin, and dried mint and stir well to combine with the vegetables. Add in the rice and season with a generous pinch of salt and pepper. Continue cooking, stirring constantly to prevent the rice sticking. When the rice starts to toast, remove from heat and stir in the fresh parsley and dill.

7. Lay the reserved cabbage leaves to cover the bottom of your large pot to stop the cabbage rolls sticking.

8. Lay a cabbage leaf on your work surface. Using a sharp knife, slice off the thick stem from the back of the cabbage leaf. Flip the leaf and spoon a tablespoon of the rice mixture on the side closest to you. Roll like a cigar. Alternatively, you can fold the leaves like a burrito. Repeat the process until you've filled all of the cabbage leaves.

9. Arrange the cabbage rolls side by side in the prepared pot. If you have any leftover filling, scatter around the cabbage rolls.

10. Place a large plate over the cabbage rolls, gently pressing them down. The plate will prevent the rolls from moving around and becoming undone. Slowly pour the vegetable stock over the plate to cover the cabbage rolls.

11. Place the pot over medium-high heat and bring the broth to a boil. Once it starts boiling, carefully remove the plate and cover with a lid. Reduce the heat to medium low and allow to simmer for 30 to 40 minutes.

12. Allow to cool for 10 to 15 minutes before serving.

SWEET AND PEPPERY NOODLE KUGEL

ORIGIN: ASHKENAZI

Traditional Noodle Kugel

Noodle kugel is a type of baked casserole made from egg noodles. It can be savory or sweet and is made with eggs, cottage cheese, and milk. Savory kugels can contain a variety of vegetables and spices.

Plant-based Noodle Kugel

This savory vegan vegetable kugel is sweet, peppery, and delicious. It has all the taste points of traditional kugel while being lighter and healthier. It tastes good hot, lukewarm, or cold. Mushrooms bring flavor and texture and, instead of dairy, silken tofu gives a creamy taste.

Plant-based Noodle Kugel Variations

- Greens: add 1–2 cups of thinly sliced spinach in step 5 to increase the vegetables in this kugel.
- Sweetness: use apricots instead of raisins for the sweet element in this kugel.

Sweet and Peppery Noodle Kugel

Prep time: 1 hour 30 minutes
Serves: 6

Tools

- Baking dish
- Blender or food processor
- Colander
- Cutting board
- Foil
- Frying pan
- Large mixing bowl
- Measuring cups and spoons
- Sharp knife
- Spatula
- 8-quart stock pot
- 9-inch round baking pan
- 10-inch sauté pan

Ingredients

- 2 cups (200 g) uncooked pasta, (farfalle, fusilli, or tagliatelle), can be gluten-free
- 3 ½ tablespoons energy egg replacer
- ¼ cup warm water
- 1 onion
- 2 cups (150 g) sliced mushrooms (button, cremini, shiitake, or a blend of the three)
- 1 cup (240 ml) vegetable broth
- 2 cups (450 g) silken tofu
- ½ cup (100 g) soft brown sugar
- ½ teaspoon salt
- 1 teaspoon pepper (more or less to taste)
- 4 tablespoons raisins
- ½ cup (65 g) breadcrumbs, can use gluten-free
- ¼ cup (15 g) fresh parsley to garnish (optional)

Instructions

1. Preheat the oven to 350°F (180°C).
2. Cook the pasta *al dente*, drain, and rinse in cool water.
3. Confirm that you have approximately 3 cups of cooked pasta and set aside.
4. Mix the energy egg replacer with ¼ cup warm water and set aside.
5. Saute the onion and mushroom in vegetable broth over medium heat for 15 minutes, adding more broth if needed.
6. Blend the silken tofu, sugar, salt, and pepper until smooth. Transfer to a large mixing bowl.
7. To the tofu mix, fold in raisins, onions, mushrooms, egg replacer, and cooked pasta.
8. Transfer to a lightly oiled baking dish and smooth the top with a spatula.
9. Cover with foil and bake for 40 minutes.
10. Remove the foil and add the breadcrumbs.
11. Bake for an additional 10 minutes until the top is lightly browned.
12. Allow to cool slightly before serving garnished with fresh parsley.

SWEET AND SOUR PINEAPPLE MEATBALLS

ORIGIN: ASHKENAZI AND SEPHARDI

Traditional Sweet and Sour Meatballs

There are many flavor variations, but the essentials of this dish are meatballs and tomato sauce. The meatballs are made with ground beef and/or ground chicken, matzah meal or bread crumbs, egg, onion, and spices. The sauce is made from tomatoes, with sweetness from any number of ingredients including brown sugar, ginger ale, grape jelly, apricot jam, ketchup, pineapple, and even Coca-Cola. Lemon juice, apple cider, or white vinegar are used to give the sour element.

Plant-based Sweet and Sour Lentil "Meatballs"

These healthier plant-based "meatballs" are made from lentils and oats or matzah meal. They are baked and served in a sweet and sour sauce made from passata, brown sugar, ketchup, pineapple, and apple cider vinegar.

Sweet and Sour Meatballs Variations

- Meatball base: replace the lentils with black beans or kidney beans.
- Sauce: for an easier sweet and sour sauce, mix grape jelly with apple cider vinegar and a touch of ketchup.
- Heat: replace the paprika with 1½ teaspoons of chili powder.

Sweet and Sour Pineapple Meatballs

Prep time: 10 minutes
Cook time: 30 minutes
Serves: 4

Tools

- Food processor
- Ice cream scoop
- Large mixing bowl
- Large saucepan
- Measuring cups and spoons
- Parchment paper
- Rimmed baking sheet
- Sharp knife
- Small bowl

Ingredients

- 1 tablespoon ground flaxseed
- 3 tablespoons water
- 1 onion, roughly chopped
- 2 garlic cloves, minced
- 2 cups (150 g) cooked brown lentils
- ½ cup (30 g) parsley, roughly chopped
- 2 tablespoons nutritional yeast
- 2 tablespoons rolled oats (or matzo meal)
- 1 teaspoon paprika
- ½ cup (120 ml) tomato passata
- ½ cup (120 ml) ketchup
- ½ cup (120 ml) fresh pineapple juice
- ¼ cup (60 ml) apple cider vinegar
- 3 tablespoons brown sugar
- 1 cup (215 g) fresh pineapple, cubed
- Salt and pepper to taste

Instructions

1. Preheat your oven to 400°F (200°C) and line a rimmed baking sheet with a piece of parchment paper.

2. In a small bowl, whisk the ground flax with the water. Set aside for a few minutes to thicken.

3. In the bowl of a food processor, combine onion, garlic, lentils, parsley, nutritional yeast, and rolled oats. Blitz until a mostly smooth dough forms, with a few larger pieces for texture. Add in the flax mixture and pulse to incorporate.

4. Transfer the mixture to a large bowl and season with salt, pepper, and paprika. Taste and adjust seasoning.

5. Use an ice cream scoop to make around 18 to 20 meatballs from the mixture and drop onto the prepared baking sheet. Roll into balls using wet hands and bake until golden-brown and crispy, around 20 to 25 minutes. Turn once halfway through the baking time.

6. In the meantime, combine passata, ketchup, pineapple juice, apple cider vinegar, and brown sugar in a large saucepan and place over medium heat. Cook, stirring occasionally, until the sauce thickens up slightly and coats the back of a spoon, around 15 to 20 minutes. Remove from heat and stir in the fresh pineapple chunks.

7. Once the meatballs are done, drop them into the sweet and sour sauce and serve 4 to 5 meatballs per portion with a generous helping of the sauce.

SWEET THREE STARCHES AND FRUITS KUGEL

ORIGIN: ASHKENAZI

Traditional Sweet Potato Kugel

Potato kugel is a baked casserole which can be savory or sweet. The typical ingredients in sweet potato kugels are grated white or sweet potatoes, flour, eggs, butter, sweet fruits like raisins or apples, and warming spices.

Plant-based Sweet Potato Kugel

This plant-based sweet potato kugel is gluten-free, dairy-free, and omits butter and margarine. It is made using three starches: grated pumpkin, white and sweet potato. There is plenty of fruit with whole apple and pear and dried raisins. Served warm, this dish has the soft, mushy texture of a pudding. After cooling for a few hours or having been refrigerated, it firms to become quiche-like, making it easy to cut into neat squares. The spices of cinnamon, paprika or chili powder, salt, and sugar enliven the sweet taste, giving the kugel a background-lingering mellow heat.

Plant-based Sweet Potato Kugel Variations

- Starch: this recipe calls for three starches. If that feels like a lot of work, simplify the dish by using just potato and sweet potato.
- Fluffy and gooey: bake the dish with vegan marshmallow on top.
- Nuts: add ¼ cup chopped almonds or pecans in step 5 to add more texture to the pudding.
- Spice: omit the chili powder to allow the paprika and cinnamon to create a milder taste profile.

Sweet Three Starches and Fruits Kugel

Prep time: 15 minutes

Cook time: 50–60 minutes

Serves: 8

Tools

- Box grater
- Fork
- Large prep bowl
- Measuring cups and spoons
- Oil spray
- Small prep bowl
- Square 9-inch baking dish

Ingredients

- 3 tablespoons egg replacer
- 6 tablespoons water
- 2 cups (120 g) peeled and grated sugar pumpkin
- 2 cups (130 g) peeled and grated russet potato
- 2 cups (130 g) peeled and grated sweet potato
- 1 apple, peeled and grated
- 1 pear, peeled and grated
- 1–2 tablespoons natural cane sugar
- 1 teaspoon cinnamon
- ½ teaspoon paprika or chili powder
- ½ teaspoon salt
- ¼ cup (20 g) of coconut flakes
- ¾ cup (115 g) raisins

Instructions

1. Preheat oven to 400°F (200°C).
2. Combine egg replacer with water in small prep bowl, mix with a fork, and set aside for 10 minutes.
3. Grate the pumpkin, potato, sweet potato, apple, and pear, and add to the large prep bowl.
4. Add sugar and all the spices and mix gently and well with clean hands.
5. Fold in raisins.
6. Lightly oil or spray the baking pan.
7. Bake uncovered for 50 to 60 minutes.
8. Allow to sit for 15 minutes before serving.

TOFU SHAKSHUKA

ORIGIN: SEPHARDI / MIZRAHI

Traditional Shakshuka

The meaning of the word *shakshuka* points to a mixture of ingredients. The dish features eggs poached in a spiced tomato sauce topped with fresh herbs. Some versions also use feta cheese to garnish. Traditionally it is served for breakfast.

Plant-based Tofu Shakshuka

This plant-based tofu shakshuka is healthy, delicious, and perfectly spiced. It is gluten-free, dairy-free, and vegan. We're replacing the eggs with a tofu mixture that mimics the texture and flavor of eggs. Serve it with a big green salad and some crusty bread.

Tofu Shakshuka Variations

- Protein: add some crumbled tempeh or mashed white beans to the tofu mixture for extra protein.
- Spices: add more chili powder or diced fresh chili pepper for more heat and spice.
- Fiber: serve over brown rice or add more vegetables, like shredded zucchini or broccoli, to the shakshuka mixture.

Tofu Shakshuka

Prep time: 10 minutes
Cook time: 30 minutes
Serves: 4

Tools

- Large oven-safe skillet
- Measuring cups and spoons
- Medium mixing bowl
- Sharp knife

Ingredients

- 1 onion, diced
- 2 red bell peppers, diced
- 3 garlic cloves, minced
- 1 teaspoon ground cumin
- ½ teaspoon chili powder
- 1 14 oz. (400 g) can crushed tomatoes
- 8 oz. (225 g) firm tofu, crumbled
- ¼ cup (60 ml) unsweetened soy milk
- 1 teaspoon kala namak (black salt)
- ½ teaspoon ground turmeric
- ½ cup (30 g) parsley, roughly chopped
- Salt and pepper to taste

Instructions

1. Preheat your oven to 400°F (200°C).
2. Add onion, bell pepper, and garlic to a large oven-safe skillet and place over medium heat. Season with salt and pepper and add a splash of water to prevent sticking. Cook, stirring occasionally, until vegetables are soft and translucent, around 5 to 6 minutes.
3. Add the cumin, chili powder, and crushed tomatoes. Increase the heat to high. and bring the tomatoes to a rapid simmer. Season with salt and pepper and cover with a lid.

4. In the meantime, in a medium mixing bowl, combine the tofu with the soy milk, kala namak, turmeric, and a large pinch of salt and pepper.

5. Uncover the skillet and spread the tofu crumble over the tomato sauce. Transfer the skillet to the oven and roast until the tofu becomes nicely golden, around 10 to 15 minutes.

6. Serve on a large platter topped with fresh parsley.

TWICE BAKED SWEET POTATO TZIMMES

ORIGIN: ASHKENAZI

Traditional Tzimmes

Tzimmes is an Ashkenazi sweet stew made with root vegetables and dried fruits. It is an extremely sweet slow-cooked savoury dish, often cooked with beef flank or brisket.

Plant-based Twice Baked Sweet Potato Tzimmes

This is a new twist on classic tzimmes: a twice baked sweet potato version. It is satiating because it is double-baked in high-fiber sweet potatoes, sweetened with natural orange juice and maple syrup. We skip the overly sweet, syrupyness of the original recipe, instead offering a nourishing and filling loaded sweet potato for a main dish.

Plant-based Twice Baked Sweet Potato Tzimmes Variations

- Add protein: add a bean like chickpeas, fava beans, or black beans in step 8.
- More sweet: add dried apricots in step 8.
- Creaminess: serve drizzled with tahini.

Twice Baked Sweet Potato Tzimmes

Prep time: 20 min
Bake time: 1 hour for sweet potatoes 15-20
Serves: 4–6

Tools

- Baking sheet
- Cutting board
- Large bowl
- Large knife
- Measuring cups and spoons
- Spoons

Ingredients

- 4 large sweet potatoes
- Juice of 2 oranges
- 2 teaspoons cinnamon
- ¼ teaspoon sea salt, or to taste
- ¼ cup (50 g) raw sugar or maple syrup
- 1 cup (125 g) prunes, coarsely chopped
- 2 green onions for garnish

Instructions

1. Preheat the oven to 375°F (190°C).
2. Bake sweet potatoes for 1 hour, or until completely baked.
3. Remove from the oven and set aside to cool.
4. When cool enough to handle, slice the sweet potatoes in half lengthwise.
5. Use a spoon to scoop out the flesh and place it in a large bowl.
6. Reserve the sweet potato skins.
7. Mash the sweet potato flesh with the orange juice, cinnamon, sea salt, and raw sugar.
8. Stir in the chopped prunes.
9. Fill the empty sweet potato skins with this mixture and place them on a baking sheet.
10. Bake for 15 minutes, until golden on top.
11. Garnish with thinly sliced green onions before serving.

DESSERTS

BAKED BIMUELOS WITH ORANGE AND DARK SYRUP GLAZE

ORIGIN: SEPHARDI

Traditional Bimuelos

A popular food eaten during Hanukkah, bimuelos are small donut balls. They are usually made with a yeast dough and deep fried, have a citrus flavor, and are drizzled in honey before serving. The basic main ingredients are oil, flour, and yeast. Many recipes use an enriched dough containing eggs and milk.

Plant-based Baked Bimuelos

This recipe is baked rather than fried, resulting in healthier, fluffy bimuelos with a crunchy exterior. Cutting the oil reduces the caloric content of these treats. Eating oily carbohydrates usually leads to sluggishness, whereas these bimuelos are easy on the stomach and give us lasting energy. As there is no frying in this version, this would be an ideal recipe to get kids involved in making. They will love seeing the dough rise and shaping their own bimuelos—but leave the syrup making to the adults.

Baked Bimuelos Variations

- Syrup flavors: swap the orange for lemon juice or blended and strained strawberry puree to create a different syrup flavor.
- Add more tanginess: add fresh lemon juice and zest to the uncooked dough.

Baked Bimuelos with Orange and Dark Syrup Glaze

Prep time: 10 minutes + 1 hour proving

Cook time: 25–30 minutes

Yield: around 16 medium-sized bimuelos

Tools

- Cloth
- Ice cream scoop
- Measuring cups and spoons
- Mixing bowl
- Parchment paper
- Saucepan
- Two cookie sheets

Ingredients

- 3 cups (360 g) all-purpose flour + 3 tablespoons
- ⅓ cup (65 g) light brown sugar
- 1 teaspoon salt
- 2 ¼ teaspoon of active dry yeast
- 1 cup (240 ml) lukewarm water
- ½ cup (120 ml) freshly squeezed orange juice
- ¼ cup (60 ml) oil for shaping the bimuelos

For the syrup:
- ½ cup (100 g) brown sugar
- ¼ cup (85 ml) date syrup
- ¼ cups of fresh orange juice in the syrup

Instructions

1. Preheat oven to 350°F (180°C).
2. Combine the flour, brown sugar, salt, and active dry yeast in a bowl.
3. Mix in the water and orange juice. Once it comes together, knead the dough with your hands for 10 minutes.
4. Cover with a damp cloth and set aside to rest and rise at room temperature for about 1 hour, or until doubled in size.
5. With oily hands, shape small balls of the dough and place them on cookie sheets lined with baking paper.
6. Bake for about 20 to 25 minutes, until golden brown in color and cooked through.
7. Meanwhile, in a saucepan dissolve the brown sugar in date syrup and orange juice.
8. Drizzle the bimuelos with the orange and date syrup before serving.

BASBOUSA CAKE

ORIGIN: SEPHARDI

Traditional Basbousa Cake

Basbousa is a semolina cake drenched in syrup. It is popular in Muslim and Jewish communities in the Middle East, North Africa, and the Balkans. In Sephardi Jewish communities it is specifically enjoyed during the holidays of Rosh Hashanah and Passover (when semolina and flour are replaced by matzo cake flour). Traditional ingredients include flour, semolina, oil, sugar, yogurt or sour cream, butter, and almonds.

Plant-based Basbousa Cake

This plant-based basbousa cake has a light and delicate crumb and is just sweet enough. Unlike the traditional version doused in a heavy sugar syrup, this cake is soaked in lightly sweetened oat milk, which gives it a moreish, milky flavor.

Vegan Basbousa Cake Variations

- Make it citrus flavored: grate the zest of a lemon or orange into the cake batter and squeeze some fresh citrus juice into the warm milk before soaking the cake.
- Make it traditional: skip the milk and use equal parts of water and agave for a syrupy basbousa cake.
- Add more texture: add up to a cup of chopped nuts or dried fruits to the cake base.

Basbousa Cake

Prep time: 10 minutes

Cook time: 40 minutes

Serves: 8–10

Tools

- Baking spray
- Large mixing bowl
- Measuring cups and spoons
- Small saucepan
- Whisk
- 8-inch cake pan

Ingredients

- 6 tablespoons aquafaba (liquid from cooked/tinned chickpeas)
- ½ cup (125 g) applesauce
- 3 tablespoons brown sugar
- ¼ cup (60 ml) maple syrup
- 3 tablespoons olive oil
- ¾ cup (180 ml) oat milk
- 1 cup (130 g) white whole-wheat flour
- 1 cup (170 g) semolina
- 2 teaspoons baking powder
- ¼ teaspoon salt

Soaking liquid
- 1 ½ (360 ml) cups oat milk
- ¼ cup (60 ml) agave
- 1 teaspoon pure vanilla extract

Instructions

1. Preheat your oven to 350°F (180°C) and lightly spray an 8-inch round cake pan with some baking spray.

2. In a large mixing bowl, whisk the aquafaba until frothy. Add in applesauce, sugar, maple syrup, oil, and oat milk. Whisk until combined.

3. Add in the flour, semolina, baking powder, and a small pinch of salt. Whisk until the flour is incorporated and the batter is lump-free. Take care not to overmix batter.

4. Transfer the batter into prepared pan and place in the oven to bake until nicely golden-brown on top, around 30 to 35 minutes. Start checking at the 25-minute mark: if a toothpick inserted into the center comes out clean, the cake is done.

5. While the cake is baking, warm the oat milk and agave in a small saucepan over medium heat. Once the milk is warmed through, remove from heat and stir in vanilla extract.

6. Once the cake is done, prick the top a couple times with a fork and pour the sweet oat milk over top. Let the cake soak for a couple hours before slicing and serving.

CHOCOLATE PRUNE BABKA

ORIGIN: ASHKENAZI

Traditional Babka

Babka is a rich braided cakey bread, similar to a French brioche but with distinctive layers of dough and filling. It is made with a sweet dough containing flour, eggs, milk, sugar, yeast, and butter. The dough is rolled and spread with flavorings such as cinnamon, apple, chocolate, dried fruits and nuts, jam, and even cheese. It is then doubled and twisted and baked in a high loaf pan to create the signature layers. A sugar syrup topping preserves moisture, and it is sometimes sprinkled with streusel topping.

Vegan Chocolate Prune Babka

This is a delicious, lower fat and sugar vegan babka. The recipe uses coconut milk to enrich the yeast-risen dough. Fat from the coconut milk makes the dough creamy and velvety, with potato puree and egg replacer providing extra stretch to give a fluffy, light texture. The chocolate filling is made with a mixture of prune paste, dark chocolate chips, and coconut milk. This babka truly is a healthier version of a decadent sweet food.

Chocolate Prune Babka Variations

- Heat: add ⅛ teaspoon chili powder to the chocolate prune filling to give it a kick.
- Chocolate: increase chocolate chips to ½ cup and decrease the prunes to ¾ cup for a richer chocolate taste.
- Crunch: add ½ cup chopped nuts and 1 crushed oreo cookie at the end of step 12 for extra decadence.
- Flax-egg: swap egg replacer for 1 tablespoon ground flax seed.
- Lower fat: replace coconut milk with plain almond milk.

Chocolate Prune Babka

Prep time: 25 minutes, plus 4 hours rising time

Cook time: 35–40 minutes

Serves: 8

Tools

- Baking sheet
- Baking sheet or loaf pan
- Baking spray
- Blender
- Large mixing bowl
- Measuring cups and spoons
- Parchment paper
- Rolling pin
- Saucepan
- Sharp knife
- Stand mixer with paddle attachment and dough hook (optional)
- Wooden spoon

Ingredients

For the Dough:
- 2 teaspoons active dry yeast
- 1 teaspoon sugar
- ½ cup (120 ml) full-fat coconut milk
- 2 cups (240 g) all-purpose flour + a bit more for kneading
- 1 tablespoon egg replacer + 2 tablespoons lukewarm water
- 1 potato, to yield ¼ cup (60 g) puree
- 1 tablespoon natural cane sugar
- 1 tablespoon canola oil
- 1 tablespoon oat milk
- 1 teaspoon salt

For the Filling:
- 1 cup (125 g) of dried prunes, chopped and soaked
- ¼ cup (60 ml) of lukewarm water
- 2 tablespoons coconut milk
- ⅛ teaspoon salt
- ¼ cup (45 g) vegan chocolate chips

For the Maple Syrup Wash:
- 1 tablespoon maple syrup
- 1 teaspoon water

Instructions

1. Soak 1 cup of pitted and chopped prunes in ¼ cup of lukewarm water and set aside until the filling stage.
2. Peel and dice the potato and place in saucepan, add water to cover the potato pieces, and boil for 12 minutes. Drain, mash with a fork, and set aside to cool.
3. In a saucepan, heat the coconut milk (for the dough) until only just lukewarm, then transfer to a bowl.
4. Add the yeast and 1 teaspoon of sugar to the lukewarm coconut milk. Use a fork to whisk together and leave to proof for 10 minutes.
5. Place 1 tablespoon egg replacer in 2 tablespoons water and mix with a fork. Allow to thicken for 1 minute.
6. Transfer proofed yeast to large prep bowl and add flour, egg replacer, potato puree, sugar, canola oil, oat milk, and salt and mix to combine.
7. Knead the dough on a lightly floured surface for 5 to 7 minutes.
8. Return the dough to the large bowl, cover, and allow to rise for 1½ to 2 hours until doubled in size.
9. Just before the end of the rising time, spray the baking sheet with vegetable oil and line with parchment paper.

10. Make the filling: blend the soaked prunes (and any liquid remaining), coconut milk, and salt until smooth and set aside. Melt the chocolate using a double boiler method (a glass bowl set on top of a pan of hot water). Add the prune paste mixture and stir together until l it forms a thick paste.

11. On a lightly floured surface, roll the dough into a rectangular shape about ¼ inch thick. Spread the filling evenly on top.

12. Roll the dough into a long roulade and cut lengthwise with a sharp knife.

13. Twist the two parts of the dough together forming a double helix shape. Place in a high loaf bread baking pan.

14. Leave the babka to rise a second time for 1½ hours, until the dough has doubled in size.

15. Carefully transfer to an oven preheated to 350 degrees to bake for 30 to 40 minutes until golden brown, or until a toothpick inserted in the center comes out clean.

16. As soon as it is done, paint on a thin layer of maple wash to add shine to the babka. Be careful not to add too much or the babka will go soggy.

17. Allow to cool for 10 to 15 minutes, slice, and serve.

CINNAMON ALMOND DONUT HOLES WITH CHOCOLATE SAUCE

ORIGIN: MODERN JEWISH LIFE

Traditional Donuts

One of the fried foods enjoyed for Hanukkah are donuts. The most popular donut is the sufganiyot. The classic ingredients are flour, yeast, sugar, eggs, margarine, and vegetable oil for frying. Traditionally, they are plain donuts filled with strawberry jam and custard after frying.

Cinnamon Almond Donut Holes with Chocolate Sauce

This recipe offers a baked gluten-free donut hole dipped in chocolate sauce. This recipe is an ideal alternative to enjoy during Hanukkah because it caters to those who cannot eat gluten and/or don't want to eat fried food. The almond and oat flour mixture creates a lovely moist crumb for these perfectly sweet, not at all heavy donut holes.

Vegan Gluten-Free Baked Donuts Holes Variation

- Peanut butter and jelly: spread ½ tablespoon of peanut butter on top of each donut hole and swirl with a teaspoon of grape or strawberry jelly.
- Sticky and sweet: use fruit jam instead of chocolate for a fruity, sticky topping.
- Powder: roll the baked donut holes in confectioners' sugar for a traditional powdered finish.

Cinnamon Almond Donut Holes with Chocolate Sauce

Prep time: 10 minutes

Cook time: 15 minutes

Yields: 8 donuts

Tools

- Cooking spray
- Donut pan
- Large spoon
- Measuring cups and spoons
- Sieve
- Small saucepan
- Spatula
- Whisk
- 1 Small bowl
- 2 Medium mixing bowls

Ingredients

- 2 teaspoons ground flax seed
- 1 ½ tablespoons water
- ¼ cup (50 g) sugar
- ¼ cup (60 ml) maple syrup
- ½ cup (120 ml) unsweetened soy milk (or any plant-based milk)
- 3 tablespoons coconut oil, melted
- 1 teaspoon vanilla extract
- 1 cup (95 g) almond flour (finely ground)
- ¾ cup (70 g) oat flour (finely ground)
- ½ teaspoon baking powder
- ½ teaspoon baking soda
- 1 teaspoon ground cinnamon
- ¼ teaspoon salt

For the Chocolate Sauce:

- ⅓ cup (60 g) bittersweet chocolate chips
- 1 tablespoon cocoa powder
- ¼ cup (60 ml) full-fat coconut milk

Instructions

1. Preheat your oven to 350°F (180°C) and spray a donut pan with some cooking spray.

2. In a small bowl, whisk the ground flax seed with the water and set aside for a few minutes to allow the mixture to thicken.

3. In a medium mixing bowl, whisk together the sugar, maple syrup, soy milk, coconut oil, and vanilla extract until smooth. Set aside.

4. In a separate medium mixing bowl, sift the almond flour, oat flour, baking powder, baking soda, cinnamon, and salt. Give all ingredients a good stir to incorporate the baking powder and baking soda.

5. Add the flax "egg" to the wet ingredients and stir to combine.

6. Gently fold the dry ingredients into the wet. The batter will be fairly thick.

7. Divide between 8 donut holes in your prepared baking pan and place in the oven to bake until a toothpick inserted into the middle comes out clean, around 12 to 15 minutes.

8. In the meantime, work on the chocolate sauce. Add the chocolate chips, cocoa powder, and coconut milk into a small saucepan and place over very low heat. Gently melt the chocolate, stirring constantly, to prevent the chocolate from burning. Once the chocolate is fully melted and the sauce is shiny, remove from heat and set aside.

9. Let the donuts cool completely before drizzling with chocolate sauce. The un-topped donuts will last for 3 to 5 days in a sealed container at room temperature.

COCONUT MACAROON COOKIES

ORIGIN: ASHKENAZI AND SEPHARDI

Traditional Coconut Macaroons

A macaroon is made using ground almonds or coconut, egg whites, and sugar. They are sometimes dipped in a rich coating of fruit jam or chocolate. Some recipes include dairy, although most are pareve. Grain-free macaroons are a favorite Jewish dessert during the holiday of Passover.

Vegan Coconut Macaroon Cookies

These delicious cookies are vegan and contain no oil, refined sugar, or gluten. They require only five simple ingredients and take no time to prepare. Double the batch if you want to make them for a family dinner—they will go fast.

Coconut Macaroon Variations

- Add more texture: stir in a couple tablespoons of chopped almonds, hazelnuts, or even dried apricots into the mix.
- Make them citrus-flavored: grate in the zest of an orange to the cookie mix and add a squeeze of orange juice to the melted chocolate.

Coconut Macaroon Cookies

Prep time: 10 minutes
Cook time: 20 minutes
Serves: 4

Tools

- Baking sheet
- Large mixing bowl
- Measuring cups and spoons
- Parchment paper
- Small saucepan
- Spoon
- Whisk

Ingredients

- ¼ cup (60 ml) aquafaba (the liquid from a can of chickpeas)
- 3 tablespoons pure maple syrup
- ½ teaspoon vanilla extract
- 1 ¼ cups (110 g) unsweetened shredded coconut
- 1 oz. (30 g) bittersweet (70%) vegan chocolate, melted

Instructions

1. Preheat your oven to 325°F (160°C) and line a rimmed baking sheet with a piece of parchment paper.

2. In a large mixing bowl, whisk the aquafaba until frothy. It doesn't need to reach firm peaks. Stir in the maple syrup and vanilla.

3. Add the shredded coconut to the aquafaba mixture and stir to combine. Take a heaped tablespoon from the mixture and form into balls using wet hands. Arrange on the prepared baking sheet. You should get around 8 medium balls.

4. Place in the oven to bake until nicely golden brown on top and around the edges, around 15 to 20 minutes.

5. In the meantime, melt the chocolate in a small saucepan over very low heat.

6. Once the macaroon cookies are done, leave them to cool for 10 minutes on the baking sheet, then drizzle them with melted dark chocolate.

7. Transfer the macaroons to the fridge to let the chocolate set for around 10 minutes.

CREAMY BERRY CHEESECAKE PARFAITS

ORIGIN: ASHKENAZI

Traditional Cheesecake Parfaits

Today, many Jewish communities eat cheesecake on Shavuot. Modern-day cheesecakes are made with ingredients like sour cream, cream cheese, butter, eggs, and sugar and can be baked or refrigerated.

Plant-based Berry Cheesecake Parfaits

These creamy, dreamy cheesecake parfaits are gluten-free, dairy-free, and don't use oil or refined sugar. They are refreshing and satisfying at the same time and take almost no time to prepare since everything is done in a food processor or blender.

Cheesecake Parfaits Variations

- Nut butter swirl: swirl a couple tablespoons of peanut or almond butter into the cheesecake before setting in the fridge.
- Tropical: top the cheesecake with some fresh mango and pineapple chunks.
- Chocolatey: add 2–3 tablespoons of unsweetened cocoa powder to the cashew cream.

Creamy Berry Cheesecake Parfaits

Prep time: 15 minutes

Refrigeration time: 2 hours

Serves: 4

Tools

- High-speed blender or food processor
- Measuring cups and spoons
- Serving glasses
- Spatula (for scraping the blender)
- Spoon

Ingredients

- ½ cup (70 g) raw almonds
- 6 Medjool dates, pitted
- 3 tablespoons unsweetened coconut flakes
- 1 ½ cups (225 g) raw cashews, soaked in water for 4–6 hours
- ¼ cup (60 ml) freshly squeezed lemon juice
- ¼ (60 ml) cup pure maple syrup
- ⅓ cup (75 g) plain vegan cream cheese (or coconut yogurt)
- 1 teaspoon pure vanilla extract
- 6 tablespoons strawberry compote (or jam)

Instructions

1. Add the almonds, dates, and unsweetened coconut flakes to a high-speed blender or food processor and blend until a dough-like ball forms. The mixture should stick together if you press it with your hands.

2. Divide the almond-date crust between four serving glasses and set aside.

3. In the same blender or food processor, add cashews, lemon juice, maple syrup, vegan cream cheese, and vanilla extract. Blend until completely smooth and creamy.

4. Spoon the creamy cashew cheesecake over the almond-date crust and place in the fridge to set for around 1 to 2 hours.

5. Before serving, top each cheesecake parfait with 1 ½ tablespoons of strawberry jam. Alternatively, mix a cup of fresh or frozen berries with a tablespoon of maple syrup and cook over medium heat until thick and jam-like.

FUDGY FLOURLESS CHOCOLATE CAKE

ORIGIN: ASHKENAZI

Traditional Flourless Chocolate Cakes

Flourless chocolate cakes are dense and rich. They are usually made with eggs, butter, sugar, and chocolate. Grain-free chocolate cakes are a modern favorite Jewish dessert during the holiday of Passover, when eating any type of grain-based leavened products is prohibited.

Plant-based Flourless Chocolate Cake

This healthier flourless chocolate cake is gluten-free, dairy-free, vegan, and insanely delicious. It is also oil-free and lower in sugar than most traditional flourless chocolate cakes. The cake is fudgy and velvety, with a slight crunch around the edges and a deep chocolate flavor.

Fudgy Flourless Chocolate Cake Variations

- Add a citrus note: grate the zest from a whole orange or 1–2 lemons into the cake batter before baking.
- Add a decorative peanut butter swirl: drizzle 2–3 tablespoons of natural, drippy peanut butter over the cake batter and swirl using a toothpick.

Fudgy Flourless Chocolate Cake

Prep time: 10 minutes
Cook time: 60 minutes
Serves: 8

Tools

- Baking spray
- Large mixing bowl
- Measuring cups and spoons
- Parchment paper
- Small saucepan
- Spatula
- Spoon
- Whisk
- 9-inch cake pan

Ingredients

- 6 oz. (170 g) dark 70% chocolate, chopped
- 2 tablespoons ground flaxseed
- 6 tablespoons water
- ½ cup (125 g) unsweetened applesauce
- 1 very ripe banana, mashed
- ¾ cup (150 g) light brown sugar
- 1 teaspoon vanilla extract
- ⅓ cup (40 g) + 2 tablespoons unsweetened cocoa powder, sifted
- 3 tablespoons ground almonds
- 2 teaspoons instant espresso powder
- ¼ teaspoon salt

Instructions

1. Preheat oven to 350°F (175°C) and grease a 9-inch cake pan with baking spray or a dab of coconut oil.

2. Place the chopped chocolate in a small saucepan over very low heat. Melt the chocolate, stirring occasionally, and remove from the heat the second it is melted.

3. Meanwhile, put the ground flaxseed in a large mixing bowl and add the water. Whisk to combine and set aside for a few minutes until the flax mixture thickens up.

4. Add the applesauce, mashed banana, brown sugar, and vanilla extract to the flax mixture and whisk to combine.

5. Add the melted chocolate to the mixture of wet ingredients and whisk to combine.

6. Add in the cocoa powder, almond flour, espresso powder, and salt. Using a spatula, gently fold the dry ingredients into the wet. The mixture will be thick and slightly glossy.

7. Pour the chocolate cake batter into a lined cake pan and bake for 50 to 60 minutes, until the top is set and the edges start to pull away from the pan.

8. Remove from the oven and leave to cool completely before slicing and serving.

9. Garnish with fresh raspberries.

"HONEY" CAKE

ORIGIN: ASHKENAZI

Traditional Honey Cakes

Traditional honey cakes include all the usual cake ingredients: flour, butter, milk, eggs ,and of course, honey. They are a popular dessert for Rosh Hashanah when honey is a symbolic food, representing hope that the upcoming new year will be "sweet."

"Honey" Cake

This sweet and soft cake is made with real, whole ingredients: a dessert you can definitely feel good about baking and eating. The cake is lightly sweetened. Using date syrup provides a true vegan version of this favorite Jewish dish. Alternatively, you can choose to stick with the traditional honey. Whichever sweetener you choose, the taste profile of this cake is similar to a spice cake and it is delicious served warm from the oven or cold with a hot cup of lemon tea.

"Honey" Cake Variations

- Add citrus: add 2 tablespoons of fresh lemon juice to the batter to add a lovely citrus note to the cake.
- Chocolate chips: replace currants with vegan chocolate chips to make for a rich chocolatey cake.
- Mini cake: use this recipe to make individual glazed cakes for your table.

"Honey" Cake

Prep time: 10 minutes

Cook time: 1 hour

Yield: one 9 ½-inch bundt cake

Serves: 8–10

Tools

- Baking spray
- Measuring cups and spoons
- Small bowl
- Small saucepan
- Whisk
- Wooden spoon
- 2 large mixing bowls
- 9 ½ inch bundt pan

Ingredients

- 2 cups (250 g) whole-wheat flour (or 1 cup whole-wheat flour + 1 cup whole-wheat pastry flour)
- 2 teaspoons baking powder
- 2 teaspoons baking soda
- ½ teaspoon sea salt
- 2 teaspoons cinnamon
- ⅛ teaspoon allspice
- 1 ⅓ (335 g) cup applesauce
- 1 cup (240 ml) non-dairy milk
- ½ cup (170 g) date syrup or honey
- 2 tablespoons fresh lemon juice
- 1 teaspoon vanilla
- 1 cup (150 g) currants

For the Glaze:
- ¼ cup (85 g) date syrup or honey
- 1 teaspoon cornstarch

Instructions

1. Preheat oven to 350°F (180°C).
2. In a large bowl, combine the flour, baking powder, baking soda, sea salt, cinnamon, and allspice.
3. In a separate large bowl, whisk together the applesauce, non-dairy milk, date/honey syrup, fresh lemon juice, and vanilla.
4. Add the dry to the wet ingredients and stir until just combined. Add the currants and stir through. Don't overmix.
5. Lightly spray the bundt pan with baking spray. Pour cake batter in.
6. Bake in 350°F (180°C) oven for 15 minutes. Reduce oven temperature to 325°F (160°C) and bake for 45 more minutes. The top should spring back to the touch when finished.
7. Cool completely before inverting onto a plate.
8. To prepare the glaze: In a small saucepan, combine the honey/date syrup and cornstarch and then whisk until smooth. Bring to a simmer over medium heat while stirring constantly. Cook for a few minutes until it thickens. Remove from the heat to cool.
9. To garnish the cake: either dust the cake lightly with powdered sugar or evenly drizzle the cake with the date/honey syrup glaze.

MALABI PUDDING

ORIGIN: SEPHARDI / MIZRAHI

Traditional Malabi Pudding

Malabi pudding is a milk-based rose-flavored pudding that is a popular Israeli dessert. The traditional ingredients are milk, rose water, sugar, and pistachio. Pareve versions of this dessert use almond or coconut milk.

Vegan Malabi Pudding

This delicious plant-based malabi is dairy-free. You'll get the creamy mouthfeel from the coconut milk and the subtle sweetness of rose water in every bite.

Vegan Malabi Pudding Variations

- Make it traditional: replace cornstarch with rice flour for a more traditional version. Rice flour will give more body to the pudding, but will also yield a grittier texture. The cornstarch makes the malabi silkier and lighter.
- Toppings: serve with pomegranate arils, fresh peaches, or persimmons cooked in sweet syrup.
- Spice: add a dash of cinnamon to the pudding base.

Malabi Pudding

Prep time: 5 minutes
Cook time: 10 minutes
Serves: 4–6

Tools

- Ladle
- Measuring cups and spoons
- Medium saucepan
- Serving glasses
- Small bowl
- Whisk

Ingredients

- 1 cup (240 ml) coconut milk
- ¾ cup (180 ml) unsweetened almond milk
- 2 tablespoons white sugar
- ¼ cup (60 ml) agave syrup
- 3 tablespoons cornstarch, diluted in 2 tablespoons water
- 1 ½ tablespoons rose water
- 6 tablespoons raspberry jam
- 6 tablespoons pistachios, chopped

Instructions

1. Add the coconut milk, almond milk, white sugar, and agave syrup to a medium saucepan and place over medium-high heat. Bring the milk mixture to just below boiling point.

2. While whisking, slowly stir in cornstarch diluted into water. Continue cooking, whisking continuously until the mixture becomes silky and nicely thickened, around 5 minutes.

3. Remove from the heat and stir in the rose water. Ladle into serving bowls and leave to cool completely. Cover and transfer into the fridge to chill for a minimum of 2 to 3 hours.

4. Top each pudding with 1½ tablespoons raspberry jam and chopped pistachios before serving.

MANDELBROT DOUBLE BAKED COOKIES

ORIGIN: ASHKENAZI

Traditional Mandelbrot

A German-Jewish cookie, traditional Mandelbrot are double baked, hard, oblong-shaped cookies made with flour, almonds, sugar, eggs, and oil. Typically they are dry and crunchy. They are often served with coffee or tea and perfect for dipping. The name "Mandelbrot" comes from the Yiddish word "mandl," which means almond.

Vegan Mandelbrot

These plant-based Mandelbrot cookies offer a tasty, lighter iteration of the traditional version. Egg replacer and ground flaxseed replace eggs and a minimal amount of coconut milk is used in place of oil. The cookies are sweet from dark brown sugar and vanilla, with a tiny amount of black pepper to enliven the taste. Adjust the texture by cutting the cookie the width you prefer: thinner for crispier or thicker for a more substantial version. Just make sure you cut them all a uniform size—if there's ever a time to use a ruler in the kitchen, this is it! These healthier mandelbrot cookies are perfect with plant-based hot cocoa, tea, or coffee.

Vegan Mandelbrot Variations

- Chocolate: add up to 1 cup vegan chocolate chips after combining the wet and dry ingredients.
- Chewy: add up to 1 cup raisins after combining the wet and dry ingredients.
- Nuts: use hazelnuts or chopped pecans in place of almonds.

Mandelbrot Double Baked Cookies

Prep time: 10 minutes

Cook time: 45 minutes

Yield: 10–20 cookies, depending on thickness

Tools

- Knife
- Measuring cups and spoons
- Mixing bowl
- Ruler
- Sharp knife
- Small bowl
- Wire cooling rack
- Wooden spoon
- 2 Baking sheets

Ingredients

- 1 tablespoon egg replacer
- 2 teaspoons ground flax seed
- 3 tablespoons water
- ¾ cup (105 g) roasted unsalted almonds
- 2 cups (240 g) flour
- ⅔ cup (135 g) dark brown sugar
- ¾ teaspoon baking powder
- ¼ teaspoon salt
- ⅛ teaspoon ground black pepper
- 2 tablespoons full-fat coconut milk
- 1 teaspoon vanilla extract
- ¼ cup (60 ml) oat milk

Instructions

1. Preheat oven to 350°F (180°C).
2. Place egg replacer and flax seed in a prep bowl and add 3 tablespoons of water. Whisk with a fork and set aside to thicken.
3. Roughly chop the almonds.
4. Mix the flour, dark brown sugar, baking powder, salt, and pepper together in a bowl.
5. In a separate bowl, combine coconut milk, vanilla extract, oat milk, and egg replacer mixture.
6. Add the wet ingredients to the dry and mix well.
7. Add the chopped almonds and mix through.
8. Form the cookie dough into a 1-inch-thick log. Divide to make 2 equal logs and place them on a baking sheet.
9. Bake for about 30 minutes, then transfer to a wire cooling rack. Allow to cool for 2 hours.
10. Cut each log into ½ to 1-inch pieces (1.3 cm to 2.5 cm) pieces (use a ruler!). Place the pieces face down on a baking sheet.
11. Bake for 10 minutes, flip, and bake for another 10 minutes.
12. Once cooled, eat immediately or store in the refrigerator for 3 to 4 days.

MINI APPLE TARTS

ORIGIN: ASHKENAZI

Traditional Apple Cakes

Apple cakes are a tradition for the holiday of Rosh Hashanah. Traditionally pareve, apple cake is dense and made with flour, baking powder, vegetable oil, sugar, eggs, apples, and spices.

Vegan Mini Apple Tarts

These vegan mini plant-based apple tartes offer a lighter apple dessert that is dairy, and refined sugar-free, vegan, and satisfying without being overly sweet. The apple flavor shines through and maple syrup brings the traditional caramel flavor to these pretty individual tarts.

Mini Apple Tart Variations

- Fruit switch: try pears or plums instead of the apples for a different flavor.
- Sour hint: add fresh cranberries and a touch of cinnamon to the fruit layer.

Mini Apple Tarts

Prep time: 10 minutes
Cook time: 30 minutes
Serves: 8

Tools

- Baking spray
- Cookie cutter

- Cutting board
- Measuring spoons
- Medium mixing bowl
- Muffin tin
- Rolling pin
- Sharp knife

Ingredients

- 4 medium apples, peeled and thinly sliced
- 2 tablespoons lemon juice, freshly-squeezed
- 6 tablespoons pure maple syrup
- 1 sheet of vegan puff pastry, thawed in the fridge overnight
- Pinch of salt

Instructions

1. Preheat your oven to 350°F (180°C) and lightly spray 8 muffin tin holes with baking spray.

2. In a medium mixing bowl, combine apples, lemon juice, maple syrup, and a small pinch of salt. Toss to coat the apples.

3. Divide the apples between the prepared 8 muffin tin holes and spoon over the maple-lemon juices, around 1 tablespoon per tart.

4. On a floured surface, roll the sheet of puff pastry to a size large enough to make 8 even circles. Cut out 8 puff pastry circles from the sheet—use a glass or a cookie cutter around the same size as the muffin tin holes.

5. Top the apples with a puff pastry lid and place in the oven to bake until the puff pastry is nicely browned and puffed up and the maple juices are bubbly around the sides, around 25 to 30 minutes.

6. Leave to cool for 10 minutes in the muffin tin before inverting on a plate. Serve the tartes with a dollop of coconut yogurt or vegan vanilla ice cream.

PEAR AND PLUM MINI FARKA CAKES

ORIGIN: SEPHARDI

Traditional Farka Cakes

Farka cake is a steamed cake made from layers of cooked couscous and dried fruits and nuts, made with sunflower oil and sugar. It is a traditional Hanukkah dessert in Tunisia.

Plant-based Farka Cakes

These healthier farka cakes are oil-free, refined sugar–free and just sweet enough. Instead of dried fruits and sugar, this recipe features freshly cooked pears, plums, and apple juice with warming spices. Cooking the fruit down with the spices releases natural sugars with delicious caramel notes, eliminating the need for added sugar.

Farka Cake Variations

- Switch fruit: switch the pears and plums for mixed berries, figs, peaches, or even pineapple.
- Size up: use an 8-inch cake pan to make one large farka cake.
- Chewy texture: add ½ cup chopped Medjool dates to add chewy sweetness.

Pear and Plum Mini Farka Cakes

Prep time: 10 minutes
Cook time: 20 minutes
Serves: 8

Tools

- Cutting board
- Measuring cups and spoons
- Medium mixing bowl
- Medium saucepan
- Plastic wrap
- Plate
- Sharp knife
- Silicone muffin tray
- Wooden spoon

Ingredients

- 2 small pears, diced
- 8–10 ripe plums, diced
- 1 teaspoon ground cinnamon
- ¼ teaspoon ground ginger
- ¼ teaspoon ground cloves
- 1 tablespoon pure maple syrup
- ¾ cup (115 g) couscous
- 1 ¼ cup (300 ml) unsweetened apple juice
- Pinch of salt

Instructions

1. Add diced pears, plums, cinnamon, ginger, cloves, and maple syrup to a medium saucepan and place over medium heat.

2. Cook, stirring occasionally, until the fruit breaks down and the mixture thickens to almost jam-like consistency, around 15 to 20 minutes. Remove from heat and set aside to cool.

3. Meanwhile, add the couscous and a small pinch of salt to a medium mixing bowl.

4. Heat the apple juice until boiling and pour over the couscous. Cover the bowl with a plate to trap the heat and steam. Let the couscous absorb the juice, around 2 to 3 minutes.

5. Line the holes of a silicone muffin tray with plastic wrap. Place a heaped tablespoon of the fruit mixture in the bottom of each, then top with the prepared couscous. Folder the plastic wrap over to cover.

6. Place the filled muffin tray in the fridge to set for a few hours or overnight.

7. Invert the farka cakes onto small plates and serve.

POMEGRANATE SORBET

ORIGIN: SEPHARDI

Traditional Pomegranate Granita

Fruit granitas are often served in Sephardi communities for Jewish holidays. It is a simple affair made of fresh ripe fruit, sugar, and water. The ingredients are blended smooth frozen, then broken up into small shards of ice crystals. This refreshing frozen dish is served for dessert or as a palate cleanser between courses.

Plant-based Pomegranate Sorbet

Sorbet is the smooth, churned cousin of the chunkier granita. This easy recipe combines the best of both: the simplicity of making granita with the elegance and pleasingly elegant texture of sorbet. This refreshing sorbet is refined sugar–free and has a perfect sweet-tangy balance from pomegranate, vodka, and maple syrup. It is an ideal make-ahead dessert and great to have on hand for a refreshing cold snack on a hot day.

Pomegranate Sorbet Variations

- Add herbs: blitz a couple sprigs of mint, basil, or even thyme with the sorbet base for a refreshing, aromatic flavor.
- Turn it into sherbet: add ¼ cup of coconut milk to the sorbet base to turn it into a creamier sherbet.
- Texture: skip the food processor step and simply break the frozen chunks into small, crunchy shards to achieve a traditional granita consistency.
- Add fiber: replace the juice with fresh ripe fruit cooked down with maple syrup, then blended.

Pomegranate Sorbet

Prep time: 10 minutes

Chill time: 4 hours

Serves: 4–6

Tools

- Food processor or blender
- Freezer-safe container
- Ice cream scoop
- Measuring cups and spoons
- Medium mixing bowl
- Rimmed baking sheet
- Serving glasses
- Whisk

Ingredients

- 2 cups (480 ml) unsweetened pomegranate juice, preferably freshly squeezed
- ⅓ cup (80 ml) pure maple syrup
- 1 tablespoon of vodka or flavored liquor (optional, but recommended)
- 2 teaspoons lemon juice, freshly squeezed

Instructions

1. In a medium mixing bowl, whisk together the pomegranate juice, maple syrup, vodka, and lemon juice.

2. Pour into a rimmed baking sheet and transfer to the freezer until completely frozen.

3. Once the sorbet base is fully frozen, remove it from the freezer and break it into smaller chunks.

4. Transfer to a food processor or a strong blender and blend until smooth and creamy. You will need to stop the processor and scrape the sides a few times.

5. Transfer the sorbet to a freezer-safe container and place in the freezer for 30 minutes or until firm and set.

6. Scoop into serving glasses and serve with fresh berries.

PUMPKIN, RASPBERRY, AND GOOEY MARSHMALLOW HAMANTASCHEN COOKIES

ORIGIN: ASHKENAZI

Traditional Hamantaschen Cookies

Hamantaschen cookies are folded in a triangle to form a pouch around a filling. The dough is made with butter, sugar, vanilla, and eggs. The filling can be poppy seed, jam, and other creative sweet and savory options. This buttery, sweet cookie is traditionally served for the Jewish holiday of Purim, as a reference to the villain Haman. Ashkenazi in origin, today these cookies are an integral part of the Purim experience all over the world.

Vegan Pumpkin, Raspberry, and Gooey Marshmallow Hamantaschen Cookies

This vegan hamantaschen offers a reduced-fat vegan cookie dough for a favorite Jewish cookie. The fillings can make these cookies a bit one-note and boring. So taking my cue from more complex tastes and sensations, I included savory pumpkin, sweet fruity dollops of raspberry jam, and vanilla gooey baked marshmallow. A note on the marshmallow: make sure to choose a vegan marshmallow brand that melts well. If they can make vegan rice crispy treats, they will work for our hamantaschen. A pecan baked on top of the marshmallow adds crunch. This cookie is fun to make and eat, and of course it is delicious.

Hamantaschen Variations

- Fruity: try using a variety of jams such as fig, strawberry, or apricot.
- Choc-nut: place chopped nuts and vegan chocolate chips in the center.
- Wild card: use the vegan cookie dough to make any type of hamantaschen you want. This dough is versatile and fail-proof.

Pumpkin, Raspberry and Gooey Marshmallow Hamantaschen Cookies

Prep time: 15 minutes

Cook time: 15–20 minutes

Yield: 20–30, depending on size

Tools

- Baking sheet
- Cookie cutter or round glass
- Fork, hand blender, or potato masher
- Large spoon
- Measuring cups and spoons
- Medium mixing bowl
- Medium saucepan
- Muffin tin
- Parchment paper
- Rolling pin
- Small bowl

Ingredients

For the Filling:
- ½ small sugar pumpkin (to make homemade pumpkin puree)
- ½ teaspoon salt

For the Dough
- ½ cup (120 ml) virgin canola or sunflower oil
- 3 tablespoons unsweetened oat milk
- ¼ cup (60 ml) orange juice
- 1 teaspoon fresh orange zest
- ½ cup (100 g) organic cane sugar
- 1 teaspoon vanilla extract

- 3 tablespoons arrowroot or potato flour
- 2 ¼ cups (270 g) all-purpose flour (or gluten-free baking mix)
- 1 teaspoon aluminum-free baking powder
- ¼ teaspoon sea salt
- 4 tablespoons good-quality raspberry jam
- 1 oz. (30 g) vegan marshmallows
- ¼ cup (30 g) chopped almonds, pecans, or hazelnuts

Instructions

1. With a sharp knife, cut half of the sugar pumpkin and bake face down on a baking sheet lined with parchment paper. Bake face down in preheated oven at 400°F (190°C) for about 40 minutes.

2. When the pumpkin is done, let it cool for 10 minutes, then scoop out flesh and mash it with a potato masher, or with the help of a hand-held blender, or just with a regular fork.

3. Season the pumpkin puree with ½ teaspoon salt and stir well and set aside.

4. Add oil, oat milk, orange juice and zest, sugar, and vanilla to a bowl and stir to make the dough.

5. Add in dry ingredients: potato starch, all-purpose flour, baking powder, and salt.

6. Stir until a soft dough forms, transfer to a working surface, and knead for 5 minutes.

7. Make the cookies right away.

8. Roll out batches of the dough ¼ inch thick between two pieces of parchment paper. Cut circles with a round cookie cutter or the top of a round glass.

9. Place a teaspoon of pumpkin puree at the center of each circle. Gently pinch the edges to form a triangle shape that forms a pouch around the filling.

10. Really pinch the three corners to create the classic hamantaschen shape.

11. Add a dollop of raspberry jam and then ½ of a marshmallow on top.

12. Place on a lined cookie sheet and bake in a preheated oven at 350°F (180°C) for 12 to 18 minutes, or until golden brown and cooked through.

13. Optional: after 10 minutes, put the chopped almonds or hazelnuts on top to toast just a bit, careful to not let them burn.

14. Optional: Dust with a little icing sugar for presentation.

STAR OF DAVID COOKIES WITH SWEET VANILLA GLAZE

ORIGIN: ASHKENAZI

Traditional Star of David Cookies

German-Jewish and American-Jewish versions of this cookie have been influenced by the Christmas cookies popular in each respective culture. German-Jewish cinnamon star cookies are made with egg whites, cinnamon, almonds, cloves, and lemon peel. The American cousin of this classic is the Star of David Hanukkah cookie, made with flour, sugar, eggs, margarine, and vanilla.

Vegan Star of David Cookies with Sweet Vanilla Glaze

These plant-based star cookies are soft in the middle, crunchy around the edges, and made with only a handful of simple ingredients. Unlike traditional sugar cookies that require large quantities of butter, these have only a touch of coconut oil as a healthier alternative.

Vegan Star of David Cookies Variations

- Citrus-flavored: add a teaspoon of lemon or orange zest to the cookie base and replace the plant-based milk with equal amounts of citrus juice in the glaze.
- Cinnamon-flavored: add a teaspoon of cinnamon to the cookie dough to create a flavor profile similar to the German cinnamon cookie.
- Slice and bake: for simpler, circular cookies, roll the dough into a cylinder, wrap, and chill in the fridge for 10 minutes. Simply slice into ¼-inch rounds and bake as instructed.

Star of David Cookies with Sweet Vanilla Glaze

Prep time: 20 minutes

Cook time: 10 minutes

Yield: 15 cookies, depending on size

Tools

- Large mixing bowl
- Measuring cups and spoons
- Parchment paper
- Rimmed baking sheet
- Rolling pin
- Small mixing bowl
- Small spoon
- Spatula
- Star cookie cutter
- Whisk

Ingredients

- 2 ½ tablespoons white sugar
- 2 tablespoons coconut oil, room temperature
- 2 tablespoons applesauce, room temperature
- 1 teaspoon vanilla extract
- 1 cup (130 g) white whole-wheat flour
- ¼ teaspoon baking powder

For the Vanilla Glaze:
- 3 tablespoons powdered sugar
- 1 tablespoon soy milk
- ½ teaspoon vanilla extract
- 2–3 drops food coloring (optional)

Instructions

1. Preheat your oven to 350°F (180°C) and line a rimmed baking sheet with a piece of parchment paper.

2. In a large mixing bowl, whisk together the sugar, coconut oil, applesauce, and vanilla extract until smooth. Add the flour and baking powder and gently fold with a spatula until a smooth cookie dough forms.

3. Chill the cookie dough in the fridge for 10 minutes to harden.

4. Roll the dough between two pieces of parchment paper to a ½-inch thickness. Use a star-shaped cutter to cut cookies from the dough. Transfer the cookies to the prepared baking sheet.

5. Gather the remaining dough into a ball and roll out again to cut more cookies. Repeat until all the dough is used up.

6. Bake until the cookies puff up slightly and turn a light golden-brown around the edges, around 7 to 9 minutes. Leave to cool completely before glazing.

7. To make the glaze, in a small bowl whisk the powdered sugar with the soy milk, vanilla extract, and food coloring if using.

8. Gently spread ¼–½ teaspoon of glaze onto each cookie. If you prefer to pipe the glaze in a decorative manner, halve the soy milk. Let the glaze set and harden for around 10 minutes before serving.

ACKNOWLEDGMENTS

Thank you to Turner Publishing colleagues Stephanie Beard and Heather Howell for believing in this book project and responding to my questions and concerns throughout the project.

Thank you to recipe testers from the Jewish Food Hero newsletter: Ethan Gross, Joe Silberlicht, Jean Vitale, Alice Chong, Neal Abrams, and Tammy Karasek. Your feedback was encouraging and helpful to making selected recipes better!

Thank you to Bonny Coombs for sharing your intellectual energy and sense of humor with me during this project.

Thank you to Rabbi Shmuly Yanklowitz for sharing ideas about the intersection of Jewish ethics and eating choices.

To my mother and father, for their unconditional love and support. Thank you for instilling in me the importance of family meals.

Charles, merci de m'avoir encouragé à persévérer dans ce projet. Ton attitude modéré envers la vie et la nourriture m'aident à poursuivre mon chemin.

Yaël, thank you for contributing your stovetop pita recipe and for cooking with me. You are my most important recipe tester. You are the Jewish girl who inspires me to create and I hope you will cherish this book as a Jewish woman.

239

The Jewish Food Hero
by Yaël Alfond-Vincent

Going Forward

If I left out your favorite Jewish recipe or if I choose recipes that you do not consider a Jewish "greatest hit," I am sorry. There are so many Jewish recipes that could have been in this book and I wish I could have included everyone's favorites.

Going forward I will be continuing my efforts of Jewish inclusiveness and diversity in future projects. I would appreciate your help with this. Please write me an email kenden@jewishfoodhero.com and tell me your favorite Jewish recipes so I can try to include your recipe ideas in a future project.

ABOUT THE AUTHOR

Kenden Alfond is a psychotherapist who started Jewish Food Hero as a community service project to support personal and environmental health. When she was 12 years old, she chose to become a vegetarian (and now is 99% vegan). She has a BA from Brown University and an MA in counseling psychology. In 2005, she went to India as an American Jewish World Service (AJWS) volunteer and went on to live and work in Afghanistan, Democratic Republic of Congo, Switzerland and Cambodia working on various projects for the United Nations and NGOs. In 2013, she obtained a certificate in plant-based nutrition from Cornell University. She started Jewish Food Hero to get healthier food onto Jewish tables around the world. Kenden is the author of *The Jewish Food Hero Cookbook and Feeding the Women of the Bible, Feeding Ourselves. Beyond Chopped Liver* is her third book.

INDEX